Misfit Leadership

LESSONS LEARNED FROM A MISFIT FBI AGENT

STEVE GLADIS, PH.D.

Disclaimer

Fictitious names of people and places have been used to protect the innocent and the guilty! Also, this book is about an era. I was an agent from 1973–1996, before cell phones, emails, or the internet were created. Finally, neuroscience tells us that memories are not entirely accurate, and eyewitnesses are often not 100% reliable. So, take this book in the spirit that it was intended as the remembrance of a misfit FBI Agent—still a misfit to this day.

Acknowledgments

Thanks to my wife, Donna, for her enduring patience and sound counsel. Thanks to Lynne Strang for her editorial expertise and sound guidance on this project. Finally, thanks to Dean McIntyre for his friendship, technical acumen, and artistic design skills, especially the use of artificial intelligence to design the cover. Thanks to Daniel Kohan of Sensical Design for his expertise and patience in making the book look great.

Copyright © Steve Gladis 2023

All rights reserved

Paperback ISBN: 978-0-9891314-9-0
E-book (kindle) ISBN: 979-8-9889394-0-5

This book is dedicated to every "misfit leader." To every fish out of water who swims funny in a school of well-behaved fish. To every leader who asks why or who dares to experiment. To every innovator in the land of if-it-ain't-broke-don't-fix-it people. I also dedicate this book to deceased FBI agent Edward Tully, who constantly tweaked the steady-state nose of law enforcement. Ed never met a new idea or an experiment he didn't like, and he has a list of accomplishments and people indebted to him that could fill a thick book. Ed took me and other misfit leaders under his protective wing when we were most vulnerable. Rest in peace, Ed, and thanks more than I can ever express.

Contents

Overview: 5 Survival Lessons from a Misfit FBI Agent   9

The Misfit New Agent   23
1   No Mustaches, Please   25
2   Welcome to La-La Land   31
3   My First Misstep   36
4   Reggie   39
5   The Underwear Man   43

The Misfit Language Student   49
6   An Aptitude Test Backfires   51
7   Butting Heads with "Professor Adolph"   53

The Misfit Field Agent   57
8   How I Started Chasing Bank Robbers   59
9   A Weird Running Routine Raises Eyebrows   62
10   Crazy Cases   67

The Misfit Headquarters Agent   85
11   Next Stop: FBI Headquarters   87
12   A Whacky Office at the Watergate   91
13   The Shark Pen   95
14   Back to La-La Land   99
15   A Silver Lining   102
16   A Fateful Pee Break   104

The Misfit Field Supervisor — 109
17 Newbies, Geriatrics, and Devoted Cynics — 111
18 A Bomber Threatens a D.C. Landmark — 115
19 Blowing Up My Career — 118
20 Fighting the System — 121

The Not-So-Misfit Academy Instructor — 127
21 Back to La-La Land Again — 129
22 Teaching Cops to Communicate — 132
23 Handling Drunks Who Don't Want to Go Home — 135
24 Fat, Dumb, and Happy — 138

The Misfit Chief Speechwriter — 143
25 Working for The Man — 145
26 The Word Whores — 148
27 Networking in the Cafeteria — 152
28 From Speechwriting to Publishing — 155
29 A Minnow Eats a Whale — 159

The Not-So-Misfit FBI Academy Unit Chief — 163
30 Back to La-La Land—This Time by Choice — 165
31 Educators Run Amok — 168
32 The Colored Polo Shirt Phenomenon — 171
33 The Commandant of Snow Removal — 174

The Misfit Agent Waves Goodbye — 179
34 Saying Goodbye Ain't So Easy — 181
35 The Last Hurrah—Party Time — 184
36 The Day After — 188

Epilogue — 191

Misfit Leadership: Key Takeaways — 194

About the Author — 204

"Until the lions have their own historians, the history of the hunt will always glorify the hunter."

—*African Proverb*

OVERVIEW

5 Survival Lessons from a Misfit FBI Agent

I have a confession to make—actually, two confessions.

Confession #1: I am dyslexic and have Attention-Deficit/Hyperactivity Disorder (ADHD). I have trouble reading, spelling, and focusing. I start too many projects at once. I misread important documents, transpose critical numbers, and make more mistakes than a drunk trying to thread a needle. Just ask my wife, Donna—thankfully, she spells her name with two n's, so it doesn't matter if I transpose them!

Confession #2: When I got out of the Marine Corps, I took a shot at being an MD, but chemistry + me did not = success. So, I then chose another career: I became an FBI agent.

It wasn't a good choice. I was a high-concept, big-picture guy who stumbled into a low-concept, detail-oriented world of evidence collection, fingerprint analysis, and meticulous documentation worthy of cross-examination in a court of law. It was where federal judges, sticklers for accuracy, frowned upon creativity and imagination, my strong suits.

And to make matters worse, I questioned the status quo. "So, why do we do it this way?" I'd ask. Or: "Have you ever tried this new way?" It was like asking the Pope, "Hey, why the funny hat?"

To add fuel to my dumpster-fire career as a "street agent," I had trouble finding stuff—a byproduct of my ADHD. During search warrants, I often missed the bloody knife, the footprints in the mud, or the burglary tools in the closet. Distracted by the art on the walls or the décor, I'd be admonished by the case agent to "open your f—ing eyes!"

In short, I was a misfit FBI agent.

But, hey, I'm hardly the only round peg who tried to fit into a square space—oops, I think I got that backward! Some of the world's best-known creatives and personalities were oddballs. In the arts, there was Leonardo da Vinci. By some accounts, he may have had Asperger's. At the very least, he could never quite fit in. Albert Einstein was bullied in school, which made him feel like an outsider. At age seventeen, he dropped out of high school. In today's world, the list of successful dropouts includes Bill Gates and Steve Jobs. And then there's Elon Musk. I rest my case, your honor.

As an FBI agent, I was a misfit in a large, bureaucratic organization that preached uniformity. People "went along to get along." In new agents training, a counselor warned me, "Sharks eat fish who swim funny. Don't swim funny!" My fellow agents were savvy enough to follow that advice. I wasn't. As a result, my tail was chewed on by more than my share of the bureaucracy's great white sharks.

Still, I managed to survive a twenty-three-year career in the FBI—and was even put in charge of several relatively important departments—mainly because I developed skills in "misfit leadership," which—for lack of a better description—I define as "leveraging weirdness or nonconformity to improve performance and character." To put it another way, I turned my oddball thinking into an asset. Thank God I did. Otherwise, I doubt I could have survived.

This book is about the career of a misfit FBI agent who would have been better off selling men's suits at Brooks Brothers. If you're seeking an entertaining read about the trials and tribulations of a guy who marched to the beat of a different drummer, you might enjoy reading my story.

On the other hand, you may be more interested in learning about misfit leadership, whose principles can be applied by leaders of all stripes and types to lead others, and themselves, better. In that case, your best bet is to read this introduction and the misfit leadership takeaways at the end of each section. You can skim the rest of the book or save it for your next beach vacation.

My thesis is simple: *Misfits can make a significant, positive difference in an organization if you bother to listen to them.* I offer these five critical lessons for leaders who want to tap their inner weirdness—or better manage the odd ducks in their organizations.

Lesson #1: Engage in Self-Learning

A big part of misfit leadership is self-learning, a practice that misfits hone through trial and error—often much error. As a kid with undiagnosed dyslexia and ADHD, I bounced around in the classroom like a ping-pong ball. But I figured out how to beat the system: I took good care of friends who could spell and had an affinity for grammar rules. In college, I wouldn't say I liked lecture classes, which, unfortunately, was the default pedagogical method back then. I slept through many a droning professor's monologue and almost dropped out at one point.

But like my fellow dyslexics, I survived by becoming a "workaround guy." I figured out, for example, that I speak better than I write. So, I started to read my writing aloud and eureka! I could hear mistakes that I often could not see. I vividly remember the release of the first spell-checking program for personal computers. When I first heard of Spell Check, I thought it was a Russian hockey player! Before long, it became like my third arm.

Later, an editor taught me another great workaround—to change the font style from Times Roman to Comic Sans before proofreading essays. It was like wearing the same suit but in entirely different colors. Errors jumped off the page like a red-haired kid in a convention of bald guys. And boy, did these workarounds, and many others, save my academic skin when I went on to get a master's degree and then my doctorate.

As we misfits use workarounds to teach ourselves, so can business leaders. Consider adding a few "misfit self-learning techniques" to your toolbox.

What misfit leaders can do:

- **Interview people.** Most creative misfits have curious minds, a good attribute for any leader. One way to stimulate your curiosity and your thinking is through informational interviews. LinkedIn is a great place to find and connect with people who have the knowledge you desire or a different perspective on your research topic. Reach out and ask for a fifteen-to-twenty-minute interview. Most people will say yes to a modest time limit. Offer to excuse yourself when you've reached the set time limit. If they ask you to stay and continue the conversation, say yes. They're interested in you, and the informational interview has just become a job interview.

- **Listen to audiobooks.** They're a godsend for those of us who have a learning disability and have trouble with written formats. For all leaders, audiobooks offer convenience since you can listen and learn from them in a car, on an airplane, or whenever you have downtime. Other non-written sources, such as podcasts and text-to-speech software, also make learning possible without dealing with reading.

- **Do the crap work.** Sometimes, what labels someone as "different" is a tolerance—or even a preference—for the work that no one else is willing to do. Early in my career, I volunteered for what most agents deemed the worst, most unnatural job: delivering suspect photos to newspapers and TV stations. This time was before email, digital photos, and (gasp) even before the internet. I learned that I enjoyed talking with the press, a discovery that led me to become a public affairs officer. When leaders step away from their desks and get in the trenches to do the crap work, they acquire information that can be immensely valuable. If you want to see this principle in action, watch an episode or two of *Undercover Boss*, a reality series that follows high-level executives when they go undercover to work in the rank-and-file of their organizations.

Lesson #2: Don't Settle for the Obvious

Just as there is more than one way to put toilet paper on the roller, there is more than one way to investigate cases, drink your coffee, or swing a baseball bat. When you're an oddball, especially one with a learning disability, you rely on your different perspective to solve problems—as you'll read in the sections of this book where I coaxed a murderer to sing, soothed a schizophrenic man by using paperclips, and trained for the Boston Marathon on my way to work to arrest bank robbers.

Throughout my FBI journey, my creative gift—developed out of necessity—helped me innovate to cope. It also inspired me to research and write a book about innovation (*Solving the Innovation Mystery: A Workplace Whodunit*, October 2016).

What misfit leaders can do:

- **Watch out for "this is how we've always done it" people.** These folks tend to be the ones who have worked in a place for a long time and find the cultural status quo to be comfortable. But it can be *too* comfortable, so people and organizations lose touch with progress. It's like that adage about boiling a frog. If the frog is put into a pot of boiling water, it will jump out to save itself. But if the frog is put in warm water, with the temperature gradually turned up, it won't perceive any danger and will be cooked to death. When the frog realizes it's in trouble, it's too late. I have often seen the human equivalent happen when people stay too long in a job or a relationship.

- **Don't rush in.** This is especially important if you're new to an organization or taking over a department. You may be tempted to shake things up when dealing with a status quo that isn't working well. But if you attempt to push change in the first thirty to ninety days, you'll learn about the enormous power of culture to reject you. I've coached too many leaders who failed to take the go-slow-at-first approach.

- **Smile.** For leaders who want to get others on board with change, my best advice comes from the title of one of my books, *Smile, Breathe. Listen.* Smiling calms people, especially subordinates who are already apprehensive. Breathing calms you down—a bit of meditation never hurts. And no one has ever criticized a good listener. Listening shows respect and elevates people. Asking for their advice or explanation about how things work offers them respect and status.

- **Think different.** Apple's legendary ad campaign gave this advice. Despite the grammatical gaff, it's genius. Likewise, a fundamental principle for Amazon's Jeff Bezos is never to stop experimenting. And remember: failure is a critical ingredient of innovation. As Bill Gates once said, "It's fine to celebrate success, but it is more important to heed the lessons of failure."

In my book on innovation, I shared this formula: Innovation = Talent + Engagement + Process. To follow the formula, hire good people who are allowed and encouraged to try, fail, and try again. Let them work on their strengths—what they are good at. Provide a supportive group that follows a process based on questions and inquiry, not cross-examination. Most importantly, please—don't settle for the obvious, the way we've always done it. Ask: "Why not try this?" Or: "What about that?" Why not sell books—and now everything—online (Bezos)? Why not produce electric cars that change the future of the entire automotive industry (Musk)? Why not invent a phone that's also a hand-held computer (Jobs)? Why not develop a computer operating system that has become the most popular one globally and the standard for most commercially available computers (Gates)?

Lesson #3: Leverage Your Strengths to Find Your Tribe

After arriving at my first FBI field office and talking to several agents, I realized that *I* was the one who was different, not them. The FBI attracts and trains some of the best people in the world, but now and then, an oddball like me sneaks in. No doubt my Marine combat experience fooled them.

Yet the same disabilities that made me a sub-par field investigator also made me a highly inventive person. Years later, when I took the VIA Character Survey developed at the University of Pennsylvania, "creativity" emerged as my number-one character strength. Simply put, I get jazzed when I'm allowed to create.

This self-knowledge was transformational because it helped me find my home: the FBI Academy, a halfway house for oddball agents and staff. What a joy to discover this Island of Misfit Toys, this place for creatives like me. At the FBI National Academy, the FBI Academy's program for law enforcement officers, people weren't afraid to question the status quo and were even encouraged to do so—primarily because of the FBI National Academy's alliance with the University of Virginia, an institution that fosters critical thinking and freedom of expression.

What misfit leaders can do:

Various well-developed assessments can help you identify your strengths, find your tribe, and bring purpose, meaning, and joy to your life. As baselines, I highly recommend these two assessments:

- **CliftonStrengths.** This assessment's founder is Donald O. Clifton, a psychologist, educator, and professor at the University of Nebraska. Clifton also was the chairman of The Gallup Organization, whose public opinion polls are among the best-known in the country. I suggest you take CliftonStrength's Top 5 assessment. At $19.99, it's the least expensive option and well worth the money. In this assessment, your top five preferences form a North Star that can guide your best career choices and uncover your strengths. When you engage with these strengths, you'll get better at whatever you're doing and love the work.

- **VIA Character Strengths Survey.** This free scientific survey (the same one I took to discover my creativity strength) was developed at the University of Pennsylvania by top psychologists Martin Seligman, Christopher Peterson, and over 50 other psychologists who participated in a prodigious effort to determine what character strengths intrinsically motivated people. In direct opposition to psychology's "what's-wrong-with-me" approach, this instrument finds out what's right with you.

In addition to these assessments, a site worth investigating is www.123test.com, an online treasure trove of free psychological tests focused on career and personal advancement.

Lesson #4: Good Stuff Can Happen from Bad Stuff

One of the worst (if not THE worst) experiences in my FBI career happened when things seemed to be going well. Then the leaders of the field office where I had been a supervisor decided to consolidate two squads—my squad and another led by my protégé. I thought it best for his career for me to leave. As a result, I was without a portfolio—and became a nomad leader.

But this bad stuff led to some very good stuff. Eventually, I got THE best job for me in the FBI—teaching at the FBI Academy. Read Sections Five (The Misfit Field Supervisor) and Six (The Not-So-Misfit Academy Instructor) for the backstory.

Once I started teaching, I asked my students to think about a low point in their lives or careers—and the path they took after that bad event. Like me, they would say, "It was the worst time in my career, but it turned out to be the best thing that ever happened."

Between my students and my own experiences, I know people can use a negative as a springboard for a positive—whether it's finding a calling, moving to a more accepting environment, meeting a spouse, or otherwise turning a life in a different, better direction. But this change doesn't happen on its own.

What misfit leaders can do:

- **Remind yourself that "This too shall pass."** Misfits are especially prone to encountering bad stuff. Understand that you may be ridiculed when you express contrarian views or propose something radical. Whatever bad stuff is happening, it's not forever. Don't let the naysayers get to you. Stay true to your core values and focus on the big picture.

- **Speak up when you need to.** You may be the lone voice expressing dissent (a common position for misfits). And yes, you face risks. As a public affairs officer in the FBI, I spoke the truth to my bosses when no one else would. As a result, I got my clock cleaned and became a member of the "out-group." This reaction told me it was time to move on, which I did. If I hadn't spoken up, it might have taken me longer to realize the toxicity of my situation.

- **Model your response after the Hero's Journey.** In 1949, Professor Joseph Campbell published *The Hero with a Thousand Faces*, which combined insights into modern psychology with Campbell's understanding of comparative mythology. The book presents a narrative template now used for most movies, books, and television shows. Under the template, known as the "monomyth" or "Hero's Journey," a hero or protagonist confronts a challenge, decides whether to take it on and then encounters adventures and perils along the way to resolution. The hero emerges as a different and better person, just as the world is better off.

This mythological framework works not only in fiction but also in real life, as my journey shows. Inevitably, every leader feels the call to adventure and must decide whether to accept or refuse that call. If you take the call, you will likely encounter bad stuff along your journey. You can choose to let adversity stop you in your tracks. Or you can choose to take it on, seek mentors who can help you navigate complex situations, tap into your courage as you step into a new world of experiences, and emerge in a different, better place.

Lesson #5: Learn How to Manage Oddballs

When people dissent, the key is not to ignore or discount them without a fair hearing. You might regret it big time.

Consider what happened in 1986 when the space shuttle Challenger exploded with seven astronauts onboard. The night before liftoff, five engineers at NASA contractor Morton Thiokol tried to stop the launch. Their data showed that the rubber seals on the shuttle's booster rockets wouldn't seal properly in cold temperatures. The January 28th launch would be the coldest one ever. Unfortunately, the engineers' managers and NASA overruled them. Not listening to the dissenters resulted in the deaths of

American astronauts, a national tragedy, and a profound setback for NASA's space program.

While most of us rarely, if ever, have to make decisions of this magnitude, it's always a good idea to at least listen to the dissenters. Sometimes they can help you see your blind spots, enabling you to reach better conclusions and avoid serious errors. And nowhere will you find a better source of alternative views than your misfits and nonconformists, who look at the world differently, sometimes upside down or sideways.

What leaders can do to help misfits:

- **Appreciate the value of misfits.** Recognize that they can be your most valuable employees if you know how to get the most out of them.

- **Invite principled insubordination.** Engage in what psychologist Todd Kashdan calls "Principled Insubordination" in his book, *The Art of Insubordination*. Such principled insubordination is a kind of deviance offered to help the greater good. We need leaders who allow dissident voices to be heard, regardless of what most people think—especially on the most critical issues. Indeed, Kashdan's research has shown if more than twenty-five percent of a group were principled insubordinates, they would most often swing the rest of the group.

- **Provide psychological safety.** In her book *The Fearless Organization*, Harvard professor Amy Edmondson has researched and written extensively about providing a safe place for people to speak the truth—especially to power. Making it okay to express what's on your mind, knowing there will be acceptance, and no punishment or retribution, allows people to speak up, even when the message is not popular but needs to be heard by the team or organization.

- **Match people with complementary strengths.** If you have a highly creative person, try to match her with someone great with details. Let the extroverts help the introverts express their views. Let the introverts teach the extroverts to listen more and talk less. Matching "yin and yang" may be a leader's most important job.

- **Respect circadian rhythms.** Everyone has an internal clock—or circadian rhythm—that affects sleep-wake patterns. Owls work better late in the day; larks like to get going early. Let people work hours that fit their circadian rhythms and watch productivity increase. As long as the work gets done, who cares?

* * *

My FBI ride was a wild one. It started and ended at the FBI Academy at Quantico because I was a misfit. If I could go back in time, I probably would have started my career as an academic and a writer instead of an agent. But it all helped to shape me, and I have no regrets.

As my experience shows, misfits see the world through a different prism. But here's the thing: Neuroscience research tells us we are *all* misfits of sorts. Here are just some of the ways we interpret our surroundings differently.

- **Sensory perception.** Due to genetics, we differ in how we perceive color, sound, temperature, and much more. For example, you may be able to interpret sound variations well but have poor visual recall. Or vice versa.

- **Attention and focus.** The brain has information thrown at it constantly, from literally millions of stimuli a day. We cannot possibly take it all in, so our brains selectively process all that data through attentional biases. This selectivity not only protects us from being overwhelmed but also influences how we interpret the world around us.

- **Cognitive bias.** Every day, we make systematic errors in judgment based on our perceptions and prejudices. Our experiences (good and bad), cultural inheritance and influences, and beliefs create our interpretation of events. "Confirmation bias" causes us to listen to information supporting our pre-existing beliefs and rejects information that contradicts those beliefs.

- **Neural processing.** Studies of Functional Magnetic Resonance Imaging (fMRI), which measures and maps brain activity, show that people process the same information differently. When interpreting sensory or intellectual data, one size does not fit all.

- **Perceptual illusions.** These work in different ways to confound your perception of reality. Optical illusions, for example, use certain visual tricks that exploit certain assumptions within human perception. One person looks at a picture and sees a vase. Another looks at the same image and sees the profiles of two faces looking at each other.

In short, our brains see the world in wildly different ways—and each of us has "a misfit streak," so to speak. If you nurture yours in a principled fashion, it will help you become a better leader. To practice misfit leadership, remember:

1. Engage in self-learning

2. Don't settle for the obvious

3. Know your strengths and use them to find your tribe

4. Understand that good stuff can happen from bad stuff

5. Learn how to manage oddballs

May these ideas enable you to tap your inner weirdness and make a positive difference in whatever you choose to do. Good luck on your journey!

—Steve Gladis

The Misfit New Agent

1
No Mustaches, Please

I came to the FBI via the "Corps," the United States Marine Corps insider name. My interest in the Bureau, the insider name for the FBI, started when I was about to get out (escape might be too strong a word) from the Corps. Don't get me wrong; the Corps taught me more about leadership—the field where I make my living now—than any university or book could ever do. So, I'm thankful—and glad I managed to live through the experience, especially my combat tour.

During those last days, I was stationed at a Marine base on the East Coast. With only a few months of military service left, I was the second-in-command of the officers' club, a holding tank for short-timers. One of our board's issues was whether to replace the silverware in the officers' dining room. I argued that many officers' wives had already "borrowed" complete place settings for eight. Changing to a new silverware pattern would encourage their fondness for a five-finger discount—and cost the club a fistful of cash.

Speaking of fists, one of my other significant concerns back then related to our informal basement bar. It was called the Ratskeller (or the "Rat," for short), a name choice no doubt influenced by some high-ranking officer's visit to Germany. The Rat, one of several bars in the club, was a popular hangout for overly testosteroned, shaved-headed, drunk junior officers. When they got to boozin', these young officers routinely punched the inert wall directly over the urinal in the head, Marine code for a toilet. Punching walls in men's rooms is a traditional, worldwide male sport, though not yet sanctioned by the International Olympic Committee.

The Rat had a men's room wall was made of plaster board that had caved like an out-of-shape, punch-drunk boxer, yielding to the he-man punches of the shaved-headed boys from the fiercest fighting machine on the earth. For a while, the gunnery sergeant in charge of the club's operations kept repairing the oft-assaulted wall—but eventually, he gave up.

When the head began to look like Dresden after the bombing, we got complaints from the occasional sober senior officer who wandered into the Rat. The complaints ended up with me as the junior officer in charge of, shall we say, "lower functions."

I pondered possible solutions. One night, I came up with an idea—or rather a research question: What would stop the fist of a drunken young Marine? How about an American flag? Indeed, no self-respecting, God-fearing, flag-waving Marine would smack Old Glory upside the head.

No, I thought. *I'd catch too much crap for using the flag to deter bad-boy behavior.*

Then it came to me in a dream, or perhaps after a bad headache: a thicker wall. So, I called the gunnery sergeant and told him to get three-quarters of an inch of marine-grade plywood, put it up in the target zone just above the urinal, and paint it the same color as the rest of the wall.

I planted myself at a small table near the head during the next happy hour. After things started, one big, young Marine, who almost had to turn sideways to fit through the head door, slammed it open with his ham-sized mitt. A minute or two later, I heard the urinal flush, then a loud thud, like a honey-baked ham slapping on the kitchen floor. Thwack! Then I heard: "Shit! I broke my f—ing hand!"

Mission accomplished.

* * *

When I wasn't thinking about such exhilarating issues as silverware and bathrooms, I thought about what I would do after being discharged from the Marine Corps. I had NO clue. But I did know that there was nothing in the want ads for an ex-Marine officer who had combat experience but still had trouble reading a map (As an undiagnosed dyslexic, I learned the hard way, in combat, that transposing numbers while map reading can be harmful to your wellbeing).

I read books about careers and leveraging my assets into a related field. My only personal assets were a college degree, a short haircut, combat experience, and the discipline to take an order, at least some of the time. With that self-knowledge, I inventoried my options.

The French Foreign Legion? No, I was not too fond of the heat.

A prison guard? I couldn't stand indoor work.

The FBI? Bingo.

I reasoned that the only difference between Marine officers and FBI agents was the cheap suits that agents wore and the white-wall haircuts that Marines sported. The fact was that many Marines and former military folks populated the Bureau.

So, I called the local FBI office and told the no-nonsense guy who answered that I wanted to become an agent. "Okay," he said, then hung up. *There was no way he could have written my name down*, I thought to myself.

Nothing happened over the next month. Finally, I gathered my courage and called again. This time, I got a friendlier-sounding guy who asked me how to spell my name, which I did (G-L-A-D-I-S). Then he asked for my *last* name after snorting a muffled chuckle.

About a week later, I got an umpteen-page application demanding excruciating details about my life—my shoe size, my Adam's apple size, and whether I'd ever had dirty fingernails. Okay, a bit of exaggeration here, but the detailed information requested by the application was extraordinary and time-consuming. It took me a month to verify the information with my mother, some of which we just had to guess at in the end.

One day, a couple of months after I sent in my application, an FBI guy showed up at my office. The agent sat down and introduced himself as Special Agent Whatever. Then he stared at me and said, "That'll have to go."

"Huh?" I said.

He pointed to my face. "That."

At this point, I thought he might be giving me a secret test to see if I could figure out code language. But the best I could come up with was another monosyllable.

"What?"

He waved his index finger repeatedly like he was analyzing a lousy painting. "The stash."

"My mustache?"

"Yep."

I was sure I had just failed my first FBI qualification test, but I promised him it was just a wild time in my life. It was coming off tomorrow morning in my bathroom sink, honestly. I noticed that he didn't take many notes that day. He left, not even leaving behind his card or a contact number.

My next contact with the FBI office was a few months later. The agent who answered the phone this time was a more likable guy. I told him I was getting married, had a job, and would attend graduate school in the fall. I'd decided to become a physician—either that or a rocket scientist. Because I could never do complicated word problems in eighth-grade math, I opted for a simpler life: to become a brain surgeon.

The friendly agent wished me luck and called me by the wrong name. I wished him and Mr. Happy, his somber partner, luck and headed to a university in the Northeast a few months later—after I married Donna, a great woman who was far better qualified than me to be just about anything, including an FBI agent.

We headed north after our honeymoon, halted abruptly by my raging case of entire-body poison ivy. We're talking about every nook and cranny of my "epidermis," as the snickering corpsman who examined me called it after he suppressed a laugh and asked, "You ARE on your honeymoon, right?"

We settled into grad-student housing, a structure that could easily pass for a modular jail cell for two. While sitting on the toilet, you could fry an egg and open the front door of our little campus bungalow.

I worked nights running a food service operation and went to school during the day while Donna worked in the school of education as a secretary—both of us envisioning my future as a surgeon saving lives and separating Siamese twins, that sort of thing.

Then one day, I came home and flatly declared, "I don't want to be a doctor." Because I had already demonstrated my capacity for both irony and practical jokes, Donna thought I might be kidding.

In my defense, I'd given the sciences a shot, worked my butt off, and decided after earning good (though not excellent) grades, I couldn't stomach four years of medical school. That's assuming I could get in—a doubtful proposition given my propensity to choke on standardized tests.

That's when I proudly offered a new career vision: "I'm going to reapply to the FBI."

"Oh," she said. Then silence.

This time, I contacted a different FBI office and got Mr. Happy's twin brother, who reactivated my application rather than making me start from scratch (thank God). Months passed as Donna tried to process the idea of not being a surgeon's wife. What truly shook her had nothing to do with being married to a surgeon but how effortlessly I could redirect my career. I'm sure she quietly hoped that my tendency for abrupt change wouldn't apply to marital matters. After all, she was a long way from home with a brain surgeon drop-out.

Later that year, we flew to Arlington, Virginia to visit my in-laws, two of the nicest people on Earth. Spending time with Donna's parents helped me understand the roots of her values, stability, and overall decency.

During the visit, Donna and I went to church with her parents on a bright spring Sunday. After the service, we were heading to the parking lot when Donna's father introduced me to a man who was an FBI agent, an "older" one who was at least in his fifties. He shook my hand and said, "I understand you've applied to be an agent."

"Yes, sir," I said in my best Marine Corps voice because the guy had short hair.

"You could have used me as a reference."

I knew this guy was influential in the FBI because Donna had mentioned him once to me, which I'd promptly forgotten.

"But I'd never met you, so…"

"I've known Donna's family for years. I'll check on your application and let you know where it stands."

"Yes, sir. Thank you," I said and almost saluted but re-directed my right hand and brushed back my hair instead, followed by a firm but not overwhelming handshake.

A week later, this FBI official sent us a pleasant, albeit formal, letter about the status of my application. "You will hear something in two weeks," he wrote.

Precisely thirteen days later, the FBI sent an acceptance letter telling me to report for new agent training that summer.

After reading my acceptance letter several times, I put it down and took a deep breath. I had proclaimed my intent to become an FBI agent. Now I was on my way, for better or worse.

2
Welcome to La-La Land

The FBI Academy lay dead center in the middle of nowhere in Quantico, Virginia. Driving through the densely wooded recesses of the Marine Corps Base Quantico, roughly the size of a European country, I had a flashback to being on patrol in Vietnam. My reverie ended when I spotted a large complex of buildings introduced by a black-and-white sign that read: FBI Academy.

In the glass-and-brick administration building lobby, which looked like a prison warden designed it, I met our new agents' counselor, "Agent Smith," a short, overweight, grinning, past-his-prime guy who greeted me with "Howdy." A pleasant fellow who dressed more like a door-to-door aluminum siding salesman than a ramrod tough G-man, Agent Smith's good-old-boy accent grated on my Northeast-attuned ear.

Other new agent candidates arrived and began assembling, forming a non-descript gaggle of cheap dark suits (mostly blue like mine). As a group, the would-be agents looked—well, frankly—out of shape. And not at all what I expected.

By nature, I'm a functional neurotic. I over-prepare for everything, driven by an innate fear of failure. So when I got word that I'd be joining the FBI—the world's leading law enforcement agency—I did what any neurotic would. I started to over-train.

I ran five to seven miles a day and did hundreds of sit-ups and scores of pushups with the kind of discipline you'd expect from a Marine, a Navy SEAL, or any garden-variety obsessive-compulsive. I also lifted weights about the rough equivalent of a house. And for laughs, I practiced holding my breath until I nearly passed out to prepare for the day we'd do drown-proofing exercises in the survival pool (the FBI would never refer to it as a swimming pool).

Indeed, people who know me well accuse me of being the kind of guy who studies for urine tests. So, by the time I set foot on the grounds of the FBI Academy, I was ready to run the Boston Marathon, which I did several years later.

All of this prepared me to train with what I'd envisioned as marble-chiseled, Greek-godlike FBI-agent candidates. Instead, what I encountered on that first day at the academy was a group of around thirty guys (no women back then), many of whom were far better prepared for a pie-eating contest at a county fair than strenuous physical exercise.

As it turned out, twenty-five of my classmates were former "clerks" in the FBI. Back then, clerks were essentially indentured servants hired by the Bureau on the wild promise that, one day, they would become agents. It was essentially a bait-and-switch program to get underpaid, overqualified people to work at administrative jobs so dull that it would cause anyone without blind faith to grind their teeth to powder in utter frustration.

Still, the Bureau allowed enough clerks to get their shot, their bite at the Bureau apple, to keep hope alive for the rest. Indeed, this group of twenty-five "clagents" (clerks-to-agents) in a single class resulted from a make-a-dream-come-true contest or a discrimination lawsuit. I can't remember which, but I do recall the word "litigation" bantered around in dorm discussions back then. Come to think of it, it was also a lawsuit that finally integrated women fully into the FBI.

Rounding out the class were the rest of us, the five "others" who had not been clerks. Three of us were close relatives or friends of important Bureau officials; two were African Americans (among the most qualified in the class). In short, we, the others, were special cases. So, there you had my new-agents class—the product of nepotism and a legal system.

The two-mile run, strategically placed at the beginning of training to scare and motivate us, was roughly the equivalent of the Bataan Death March for many of my classmates. When we lined up to run, I was ready with a plan.

As an experienced runner, I edged my way to the front of the gym-shorted and tee-shirted guys, most of whom looked like prisoners who'd just been given their inmate uniforms and were wearing them for the first time. Many looked like it was the first gym gear they'd worn since receiving "atomic wedgies" (Google it) from the football jocks in high school.

The voice of Agent Smith twanged: "Gintlemen, take your marks, git ready, git set, go!"

Sporting a pair of Tiger running shoes, I took off like a shot and never looked back until the first turn-around point at roughly three-fourths of a mile. When I did look, only one guy—another special (non-clerk) agent candidate—was within one hundred yards of me.

But after him, it looked like a neutron bomb had hit: bodies strewn up and down the steamy, hot-tarred road, some still running, others in various states of delirium. Some guys tossed their cookies on the side of the road; others wandered disoriented. Not a pretty sight.

I kept running and crossed the finish line, then waited and cheered the rest who finished in what felt like enough time to allow me and a few others to put a serious dent in reading *War and Peace*.

* * *

While I had an advantage in the fitness department, academics were another matter. Much of the academy's curriculum focused on "field office communication," a subject that most of my classmates understood from years of FBI employment. The importance of this administrative training, where we shuffled endless pieces of colored paper and forms, was etched in our brains by an instructor who showed us a slide of a young boy on a toilet reaching for the toilet paper with the caption: "It ain't over 'til the paperwork's done." I later came to think of the FBI as the Federal Bureau of Incessant paperwork.

If I struggled anywhere in training, it was among the limitless FBI forms and black three-hole punches, which were office essentials in the pre-automation era. The sheer boredom nearly drove me to the priesthood, where I reasoned memorizing Latin had to be more interesting.

But soon, we also studied federal law, criminal investigative procedure, handcuffing and arrest techniques, and practical solutions to common law enforcement challenges. Of all the skills we learned, firearms was the most fun and, statistically, the least likely to be needed daily, as I would discover later in my career.

A firearm—the equalizer that helped settle the West—allows anyone to take on any foe with the help of a single propellant that explodes out of a gun barrel. Unlike our British ancestors, who opined that guns killed bad guys and good guys alike and were better left universally banned, Americans have embraced firearms with all the enthusiasm and promise of a wino unscrewing a bottle of cheap wine. Passed in 1789, the Second Amendment (the right to keep and bear arms) was more likely enacted to protect slave owners from plantation revolts than to protect innocent tourists from getting mugged while unwittingly wandering into a crime-ridden section of a big city.

So law enforcement, the referee of our gun-drunk society, reasoned that it needed at least as much firepower as the gun-packing wackos wandering the streets. Since my combat experience, I'd struggled with the original American rationale for firearms but found no fault with law enforcement's extended reasoning.

Indeed, as an FBI agent, self-protection was a concept I could heartily embrace. And embrace it, I did. I shot well, tearing the hell out of silhouette targets and pop-up cardboard figures of bad guys with gruesome, cartoonish faces needing a shave. But following combat, I was fully aware that blasting away at cardboard that never blinked was a hell of a lot different than pulling a trigger on a flesh-and-blood human.

Most of my class thrived in firearms. The guys in the worst physical shape did exceptionally well, or so it seemed to me. They also excelled in another area: they knew how to "go along to get along."

In the FBI, this skill was critical—and one that I lacked as I was about to find out.

3

My First Misstep

Near the end of my FBI training, I discovered what many lawyers learn during their first year of law practice: the training was much more fun than the actual job. I also found that my intuitive personality differed significantly from most FBI agents, who were as literal as my tax accountant.

This revelation came to me during, of all times, my first tour of FBI Headquarters in Washington, D.C. When our group of trainees reached the FBI's central file center, we met "Clyde," a gloating bureaucrat who nearly burst with pride as he showed us a card catalog system that would have made any horned-rimmed librarian salivate.

"We have THE most extensive reference system in THE WORLD," said Clyde, uttering these words as if he were describing Moses coming down from the mountain with the tablets in hand. He glowed with sanctimonious radiance, not unlike a fundamentalist preacher talking with absolute certainty about the afterlife.

My heart sank like a rock. *Holy cow*, I thought. *A hand-search, card-index file was at the core of the leading intelligence agency in the world?* I felt like Dorothy in the Wizard of Oz when she discovered the true identity of the Wizard. What about automation? Yes, this was way back when, but IBM had developed early systems to sort information punch cards quickly. Surely, these guys had heard of computers. Surely.

Clyde bragged about the number of cards in his system, how many new ones came in a day, and how many criminals they'd caught due to the fast-fingered file clerks sorting through bazillions of index cards. Then he asked if we had any questions.

Asking for questions during training is like asking someone, "How are you?" For example, you don't want to know that the person has a nasty sinus infection. The inquiry is merely pro forma. So, Clyde started to turn away, presuming no questions would be forthcoming.

God has blessed me with many things, but discretion sometimes eludes me. As Clyde turned back to his revered index cards, I could not resist.

"What about using computers?" I asked.

Clyde froze. He looked at my counselor, Agent Smith, who did a double-take. Far more savvy in such situations, my classmates remained silent, looked down at their shoes, and edged away from me. Time went into slow motion, like during a car crash or when you were swimming underwater.

Clyde looked my way and said, "We think this system works quite well."

And that was my epiphany. I realized I had just farted in church loud enough to be heard by the whole congregation.

A quiet hush descended. As our red-faced counselor ushered the class to the next of many experts we'd meet that day, he pulled me aside and advised me to listen more and talk less.

He didn't have to say another word. I got it. Twenty years later, my counselor's warning would be articulated more elegantly— though no less thoughtfully—by an FBI Academy instructor who gave his new agents class this advice:

"Sharks eat fish who swim funny. Don't swim funny."

* * *

Despite my misstep, I managed to get through new agents' training. Back then, graduation from the FBI Academy was one step above elementary school graduation. My very pregnant wife, Donna, attended the modest ceremony with her parents as I walked across the stage and got my credentials—the most prized possession of an FBI agent.

After the excitement dwindled from the graduation, which we thought fully empowered us to arrest people and use firearms, we were told to get out of town by sunset—mainly, I suspected, so Agent Smith could clear us off his dance card and welcome the next group of recruits with his signature greeting, "Howdy."

4

Reggie

Most agents remember their first case, first arrest, first trial, and first conviction—usually with affection unless it involves an in-law or former friend. Likewise, every new agent's first office is unique. It's a lot like the first girl or guy you ever kiss. In my case, the first girl; I'm not admitting to any more than that.

Oddly enough—which accurately summarizes my entire out-of-step career with the FBI—I had three first-office experiences. The first happened when Donna was eight-and-a-half months pregnant with our first child. Because of her condition, the FBI allowed me to stay put and work temporarily at a local field office near where we lived after graduation.

After a weekend of cleaning my already immaculate gun, practicing how to flip open my creds, and looking in the mirror with as stern a face as I could muster, I headed out for my first day on the job. My office was located in an old, stately building. Inside, it looked like a medieval castle or a dungeon—something you might expect in Eastern Europe before the Berlin Wall came down. I took the creaky elevator to the eighth floor on that first day.

When the elevator door clanked open like a B-class horror movie, I stepped out and saw a sea of steel-gray government-issue desks and chairs. Some of the more luxurious ones swiveled and could be adjusted if you had about an hour and weren't afraid to get your hands dirty.

At one desk, an overweight guy sat with rolled up-sleeves, no doubt to deal with the poorly ventilated space's stuffiness and the heat radiating from the seven ancient floors below. He was a decent enough fellow who gave me general instructions, most of which recognized my temporary status. He also dispensed a piece of advice delivered with reverence, as if he were giving me the secret code number that got me into the FBI vault: *"Don't embarrass the Bureau."*

I nodded reverently as he handed me a folder containing a bundle of serials—FBI talk for papers, usually related to a case—with action items that were already past due.

While I'd wished for some dangerous fugitive or extortion cases, my initial ones were applicant cases. My first "big case" centered on John Smith from somewhere in Illinois, Iowa, or maybe another state that begins with the letter "I," who wanted to become a government employee. I had—metaphorically speaking—gotten ready for the big dance but found it taking place in a closet.

To help me adjust, I was assigned a mentor. Every new agent gets one—a seasoned FBI agent who keeps you from embarrassing the Bureau. Generally, the mentors consisted of two types of senior agents. The first group was the guys close to retirement, who were far more interested in reading *The Wall Street Journal* than the latest behavioral science journal of abnormal criminal psychology. The second was newly transferred-in agents from other offices. Back then, the Bureau's agent-rotation policy moved experienced agents from small offices to top-ten offices—the ten largest cities in the country.

My mentor was "Reggie," a top-ten transfer with fire in his belly. Reggie talked faster than a chipmunk on speed and had a coffee cup perpetually clutched in his right hand, as he did that first morning when we met in my supervisor's office. Later, we sped off in a Bureau car to begin my field orientation—at a local donut shop.

Picture how a frantic squirrel during the fall-nut-hunting season might drive, and you'll have a fair idea of what it's like driving with Reggie. He grew up in a big city but fancied himself as a professional race car driver. Like a manic depressive in a manic phase, Reggie constantly ingested caffeine, talked incessantly, and gave bursts of advice—all punctuated by epithets and curses that he hurled at other drivers.

Much of my training covered Reggie's leads as mine gathered moss. Whenever we arrived at a house, he'd screech up to the curb, scan the piece of file paper with background info on the applicant, then bound up to the front door with me trying to keep up. He pounded so hard on the door that I was sure he'd damaged the wood or his hand.

If a woman opened the door, he'd flash his creds and say:

"Hello, Ma'am. Did you know that John Smith has applied for a position within the federal government?"

Woman: "Yes. Won't you come in?"

Reggie (Now speaking so fast that he sounds like a telemarketer who no longer stops at the periods): Ma'am,couldyoucommentastothecharacter,associates,reputationandloyaltytothefederalgovernmentofthisperson?"

Woman: "What?"

Reggie (Slowing to slightly below supersonic speed, repeats): "Could you comment on the applicant's character, associates, reputation, and loyalty to the federal government?"

Woman: "Well, yes—good character, excellent reputation in the community, fine friends, and I guess, why, of course, loyal to the country," she might say, no doubt wondering what the hell loyalty to the federal government meant other than being forced to pay taxes.

Reggie would make two or three cryptic notes, say "Thank you, Ma'am," spin on his heels like he was on the U.S. Marine Corps

Silent Drill Team, and exit stage left faster than a speeding bullet, leaving in his wake a woman who wanted to chat and maybe ask what it's like to be an FBI agent.

A couple of weeks of Reggie's training was about all my caseload deadlines could bear. So, I began my second phase of training—Reggie avoidance. Before daybreak, I got into the office, snagged a set of car keys, and bolted for the door before Reggie opened his eyes and tried to whack the snooze alarm next to his bed. I hit the streets so early that I woke up many interviewees on more than a few occasions. In a week, I was caught up on my cases and pestered my supervisor for more work.

Of course, giving the brush-off to Reggie required a set of excuses. First, I told him I was a hopeless insomniac—true—, so I retained my honesty. Later, I told him I was a loner, which was less accurate but provided plausible cover. I'm sure I wasn't the first new agent to give Reggie the slip. I still wonder if the supervisor didn't use Reggie as his secret weapon to increase office productivity.

5

The Underwear Man

Five weeks after I began my education under Reggie, Donna delivered our first daughter. Then we were off to the second of my first offices, which was located in a large, sprawling city in the Midwest. The move was in January, not exactly the best time to drive to that part of the country. It was snowing like hell and felt more like Alaska.

I had called my new office to get a recommendation for a safe, reasonable hotel, emphasizing reasonable since I now carried a legal weapon (and had more firepower than money). Following the unflinchingly confident advice from the office, we pulled up to a place that looked like a hooker's flop. But the price was right—for the room, I mean. Without realizing it, I first saw the "good-deal" mentality of FBI agents, who would walk a mile to save a buck.

Based on my combat experience, I was assigned to a criminal squad, a real-live FBI squad where we chased fugitives and not applicants. *At last*, I thought: *The real FBI.*

And, indeed, it was. We chased after guys with rap sheets longer than the screen credits for *The Godfather*. I had a blast. I was in the office at the crack of dawn, worked until dusk, and would have worked even longer hours had I not been partnered with "Jack."

Jack was a family guy whose brain had a "back-to-normal" switch. He knew when to turn it on and go home. I did not. Jack helped me remember that I had a wife and a colicky newborn cooped up in a hotel room.

It wasn't that I was uncaring but instead obsessed—not an isolated experience in my life. But somehow, I always managed to surround myself with people like my wife and Jack, who became my non-prescription Prozac.

My first arrest case of anyone potentially dangerous happened during this period in my career. Jack and I were stalking one of his fugitives, "Gerald," a parole violator who needed scooping up.

We approached an unglamorous home in a rundown section of town, with burned-out cars on blocks, road kill, and houses with more locks on their doors than a maximum security prison.

Before we rolled up to the house of the fugitive's mother, Jack reviewed the facts of the case and gave last-minute instructions. He'd handle the intros, and I should watch out for Gerald—Jack said this as he showed me a photo of a kid who looked like two-thirds of the city. I glanced at the picture and said, "Sure," like I had a clue that I could pick this kid out in a crowd of one.

After determining we were FBI agents and unlocking a six-pack of armor-resistant steel locks, a woman in her fifties, who looked like she'd just rolled out of bed, opened the reinforced door.

"Hello, ma'am, I 'm Jack, and this is Steve, my partner." Jack had the introductory credential-flip perfected to professional elegance. Jack was calm, no question about it.

"Is Gerald staying here?"

Without saying a word, she pointed up some stairs leading to darkened bedrooms on the second floor. Jack nodded, and I tried to simulate the nod, but it came out like I'd just been rear-ended in a car. She understood I was a beginner by the way she nodded back.

Up the dark stairs, we climbed, both of us with our hands on our revolvers—no Glock 9mms back then. After our eyes adjusted to the darkness, Jack made his way to a bed in the first room. Gently but firmly, he woke up a young twenty-something kid who stood with early morning embarrassment in his Jockey shorts in front of two guys in suits.

"Are you Gerald?" Jack asked.

"No," the young man replied. Then he pointed conspiratorially to the back of the deep shrouded room.

"Keep an eye on him," Jack said to me, which I did. The underwear-clad young man slowly walked downstairs; I figured to pee or get coffee. I watched him to ensure he didn't return with a weapon or some friends to help him.

Then oddly, I saw him open the front door, still wearing only his underwear, even though it was a bitterly cold January day. *Maybe he's grabbing the paper*, I thought. Then I watched him sprint down the icy street, barefoot and in his Jockey underwear. I remember thinking; this is bizarre behavior. He ran a little like Carl Lewis and other Olympic sprinters I'd admired, but it had to be cold.

Jack came back. "Where's Gerald?"

"Who?"

"The guy I asked you to watch."

"The guy in his underwear?"

"Yep."

"I did watch him. He descended the stairs, then took off running down the street—in his underwear."

"Great," Jack said.

To his credit and my undying thanks, Jack never used this rookie mistake to get a rise from the rest of the crusty squad agents, who surely would have lapped up this story with a spoon. Two weeks later, we came back and grabbed Gerald. When we did, Jack smiled at me but never said a word. We'd meet again many years later when he was my FBI Academy boss. I consider myself lucky to have worked with him twice in my career.

During that exciting and busy time, I was exhausted when I finally made it home at night to our efficiency apartment—a room about the size of a phone booth with a hotplate. Before falling asleep in my soup, I made what felt like Promethean attempts at conversation with Donna, who tried to keep our bawling daughter from waking up the dead in the local cemetery.

In retrospect, this was one of the most selfish periods of my life. I had the time of my life while Donna was a prisoner in place at the social level of Alcatraz, where her only two daily interactions, other than with my soprano-screaming daughter, were with a mouse who visited for scraps and the "maid" who tossed new sheets and towels into our hotel room on a semi-periodic basis.

This living situation wouldn't last, however. An unexpected phone call was about to change the direction of our lives.

The Misfit New Agent—Key Takeaways

Don't sweat the small stuff. Back when I was applying for the FBI, a small thing (my mustache) would have become a big thing if I hadn't shaved it off. Today, tattoos, multiple body piercings, and other displays of individuality have become more common in the workplace. Expect creative people to display their individuality and develop a policy that makes sense for your organization.

Watch out for rote onboarding. After a few dozen (or maybe a few hundred) briefings, people in charge of training can go on autopilot, like my bureaucratic "friend" Clyde. Encourage your trainers to exercise their inner weirdness and inject creativity into the onboarding process to keep it from getting stale.

Pair oddballs with mentors who "get" them. My partner Jack had no idea that—like many dyslexics—I tended to have a literal way of thinking. So when he asked me to "keep an eye on" the underwear man, that's precisely what I did–even as he sprinted barefoot down the street! To his credit, Jack laughed it off, and we developed a good relationship that lasted for many years.

The Misfit Language Student

6

An Aptitude Test Backfires

Eventually, Donna and I left the efficiency apartment and moved into a respectable townhouse in a well-groomed suburban neighborhood. Within three months, we finished hanging our last pictures, almost precisely when I got a call from FBI Headquarters.

Due to a policy change, the powers that be were looking frantically for agents to go to language school. My cigar-smoking—and now incredulous—supervisor summoned me to his office and asked about a communication he'd also received about my possibility of attending language school. He noted that my "selection" resulted from a high score on a language aptitude test I took during new agent training.

In the first week of this training, administrators throw roughly thirteen thousand pieces of paper for you to sign—forms for health insurance, life insurance, disability insurance, survivor benefits, and next-of-kin notification all get pushed in front of you as part of the necessary administrative rigmarole.

New agents also undergo testing in every bodily and mental function you could imagine. Cardiac stress tests. Psychological tests. Mental tests. Fitness tests. Blood and urine tests. If something, anything, could be tested, the FBI did.

Among the deluge of tests was the infamous language aptitude test. The more experienced clagents (remember these clerks-to-agents) knew what a good score on the language test meant: an instant assignment to a top-ten office in a big, high-cost-of-living city. Back then, there was no increased pay differential; agents in New York City received the same pay as agents in Akron, Ohio. In short, language school could be a one-way ticket to bankruptcy reserved for naïve newbies like me or for agents in bad offices who hoped to escape to another, not-as-bad office.

Of course, the clagents failed to share this vital information with the rest of us new agents. So, I took the test and tried my best, like I did for the two-mile run. The result: when our counselor announced our test results in class, my nose-bleed-high score raised everyone's eyebrows.

Thus, the phone call from FBI Headquarters. Did I want to study one of several languages considered vital to the FBI? Not knowing any better, I said, "Sure." Language school sounded good, especially since it was in a much warmer climate than the ice freezer where I lived back then.

While I beamed with a misguided sense of accomplishment, the clagents snickered as if I had just unwittingly volunteered to be a javelin catcher at the Olympics. It didn't take long for them to lay down money on which financial hellhole of a city I'd end up assigned to when I graduated from the language school.

If my naiveté wasn't bad enough for me, I convinced my friend "Sam," another new agent, to join me on the adventure. Sam called headquarters and learned that he, too, had done well on the language test. Somehow, they'd overlooked his score and thanked him for calling.

Less than two weeks later, Sam and I drove cross country to foreign language training, the third of my first-office experiences. Upon arrival, we got settled and arranged for our wives to fly out and join us—the two budding linguists.

7
Butting Heads with "Professor Adolph"

The language school was located at a military base on the West Coast. The instructors were expatriates who taught their mother tongues. In my case, that meant an Eastern European language since my training was during the Cold War.

Imagine taking dance lessons from guys with all the social charm of a German general in a World War II movie saying: "Vee have ways of making you learn, Herr Smith … .vee haf our vays." I know it's unfair to compare these instructors to German generals, but I want to convey the mentality and atmosphere these almost-all-male expats created.

My class had only four students. Four! Sam, studying another language, was in a class with a similar headcount. For both of us, the ultra-small class size meant no escaping into the crowd when you didn't study your vocabulary—no hiding behind the hulking, shadow-casting football player in the fifth row. Unlike my old college days with approximately seven hundred sleeping students in a lecture hall, skipping class and not having your absence noticed was impossible.

Also, this was a military school that favored jackbooted academics. Envision a university that allowed everything short of physical torture—including inhumanely boring classes and insane homework assignments. Had I worked this hard in college and grad school, I might have been short-listed for the Rhodes Scholarship.

My instructor, "Adolph," was a stiff-backed hombre with a fiercely trimmed mustache and smoked unfiltered Camel cigarettes. Adolph expected perfection and cracked a stinging academic whip—he slammed a long wooden pointer on the not-so-stylish, post-World-War-II vintage classroom furniture, the kind you might have seen in 1940s propaganda news clips that showed our GIs getting vital training before they were shipped to Europe to fight the Huns. I'm mixing metaphors here, but you get the picture—in black and white.

Our class consisted of two FBI agents, two soldiers, and Adolph, who strutted just this side of a polite goose step with his pointer under his armpit at the ready. Every night, we had to memorize roughly three thousand words. Okay, maybe it was twenty-five or thirty words, but it was still a bunch.

We also had to translate endless pages of English into our newfound tongue and prepare each night for the next day's six hours of interrogation, conducted by a guy who received his pedagogical techniques from the Marquis de Sade. As he strutted around the room, Adolph terrorized the class with, "Vat does dis mean? Tranzlate dat, Vat your zaying? Zay dat again."

Day after day, he beat on us like he was breaking prisoners of war. Sometimes I thought I heard a dentist's drill in the background. Intuitively, I knew Adolph wanted to toughen us for the big game, but he was way over the top.

One day, after he'd ridiculed me even more than my former Marine Corps drill sergeant, I stood up and walked toward the classroom door.

"Ver are you going?"

"Out."

"Der claz is not over."

"Later, Adolph."

So, I went for a valk and das coffee. Later that day, I returned, and Adolph and I had a sit-down meeting. I said I would leave school if he didn't improve his general treatment of the class and me.

He reminded me that this was the military, and he "vas das leader." I reminded him I was not in the army and could quit whenever I wanted—explaining the basic notion of freedom, which I was sure he knew intellectually but never had adopted its basic tenants in his classroom.

I further suggested that, if I did leave, I would document my classroom experience in excruciating detail and send it to the most liberal national periodical I could find. Adolf masked the terror in his eyes by taking a long drag on his unfiltered cigarette.

We came to a kind of truce—more like peaceful co-existence. I did the best I could to wrestle with the language, and Adolph did the best he could with me. Neither he nor I was perfect, but I tried harder not to walk out of his class, and he walked a wider, softer arch around the classroom. When I finally graduated, we shook hands like two bloody prize fighters do after pummeling each other around the ring for an everlasting fight.

One single bright spot of my language school experience almost made it worth the daily academic floggings. We were allowed two hours for lunch to eat and exercise. To fill the void, I started running again, which helped me cope with six hours of grueling training each day, followed by three hours of homework each night.

I ran and ran. Before long, I'd run myself straight into a few marathons—a form of athletic masochism that was the physical equivalent of our daily six-hour academic marathon with Adolph.

My marathon training went far better than my language training. So much better that I decided to enter the Boston Marathon. My unconventional training for this endurance test would occur at my next assignment, which—as every clagent in new agents training had predicted—was in a big-city office.

The Misfit Language Student— Key Takeaways

Discourage groupthink. Groupthink happens when people who desire conformity make decisions without discussion or deliberation. That's basically what the "clagents" did when, as a group, they concluded that language school was a bad deal. To make matters worse, they kept their conclusion to themselves, which resulted in any dissenting agents (like me) unknowingly becoming misfits. Had their bosses intervened (or at least cared), this mindset could have been disrupted—and the language school might have been able to recruit more candidates.

Respect contrarians. I was one of the few agents who wanted to attend language school. I want to think that I showed a willingness to serve at a time when the FBI urgently needed foreign language proficiency. Appreciate the people in your organization willing to go against the grain and do what others don't (or won't) do.

Get to the root of head butting. When disputes arise between misfits and their bosses or coworkers, don't assume the problem rests with the misfit. In language school, I confronted "Professor Adolph" because I couldn't tolerate his sadistic treatment of the class and me.

The Misfit Field Agent

8
How I Started Chasing Bank Robbers

My new field office was my fourth office, but I think of it as my real first office. That's because, despite a couple of years or so in the FBI, I'd never had the primal first-office-agent experience I described earlier.

When I arrived, it was late May, and the winter snows were finally melting in this Midwestern city with supersonic winds off a Great Lake. Later that fall, when the first ice crystals etched deep red, frostbitten groves in my cheeks, I would curse my clagent classmates who scored low enough on their language school tests to avoid the location where I had landed. I fantasized about stalking each of them and stuffing a five-pound bag of ice cubes into their shorts as they slept.

Because of my training in language school, I was assigned to a squad that investigated matters requiring proficiency in the Eastern European language I could supposedly speak. It was pretty dull stuff and, as far as I could tell, a cerebral assignment. I felt like a research librarian whose desk was in the infield of the Kentucky Derby—the wrong guy in the utterly wrong place.

To add to my poor fit, I was placed under the mentorship of a guy who was more interested in where he ate lunch than his cases. So, I slipped him and began to chase bank robbers. This era was when bank robberies were a bigger deal to the FBI and before all the terrorists I would encounter later in my career.

* * *

Long ago, here's how it went down when a bank got robbed: The FBI field office issued a radio alert to all nearby agents, asking them to respond immediately to help cover the rapidly growing number of leads. The more people you throw at one of these crimes, the better your chance of solving it quickly.

Some near-retirement agents saw the call as a rude interruption of their daily routine. But for me, it was salvation. I decided to respond to every bank robbery. My rule: if I picked it up on my FBI radio, I was on the hunt no matter how far away the robbery was.

I also volunteered for all the crap work, becoming the moral equivalent of an investigative hooker. I dusted large and small banks for fingerprints until I looked like a chimney sweep who'd had a rough day. I canvassed some of the ugliest streets in America, talking to every person within miles of the robbery until my feet had blisters or my pen ran out of ink. I took the bank surveillance film to be developed and hung around for hours until a guy who looked like The Hunchback of Notre Dame finally emerged with the grainy, black-and-white prints of the bank robbers.

I even volunteered for what most agents deemed the worst, most unnatural job: Delivering suspect photos to newspapers and TV stations.

I soon learned that this assignment was the valor equivalent of volunteering for a medal-of-honor-worthy combat assignment—so great the agents' fear of talking with the media. After many rather enjoyable chats with the press corps, I realized, yet again, I was a misfit FBI agent.

But I never let on that I liked these reporters and editors. Instead, I grumbled and complained while secretly looking forward to seeing my new media friends. As for the press folks, it delighted them to interact with an FBI agent who gave them helpful information rather than the usual, terse "No comment."

My constant presence at bank robberies eventually earned me a transfer to the bank robbery squad. In addition, my willingness to put myself at continuous mortal risk got me appointed as the field office's media liaison and earned me deep condolences from the other agents in the office.

By now, I had learned that, in the Bureau, you should never act like you enjoyed something, or they'd assign you to something else. It was a kind of reverse psychology, a mentality that somehow reasoned that an agent could not be productive unless, like an artist, you suffered.

9

A Weird Running Routine Raises Eyebrows

At the same time that I joined the bank robbery squad, I decided to train seriously for the Boston Marathon taking place that April. Unfortunately, work got in the way.

I worked ten to twelve-hour days and commuted for another hour or so. This schedule barely allowed enough time to eat, sleep, and see my family, let alone train for a highly competitive race. So, I decided to run to work, which confirmed my insanity to everyone in the office.

To implement my marathon-training regimen, I had to overcome some logistical challenges. I devised an elaborate—but ultimately effective—plan that made me look like a complete lunatic, especially to my more conservative FBI colleagues.

Every Sunday night, I hauled a week's worth of suits, shirts, ties, shoes, socks, and underwear into the office. In the basement of our federal building, I found an abandoned shower used to store toilet paper that I moved and restacked in a more suitable space. After installing a new shower head and curtain, I scrubbed the early nineteenth-century tile to the point of bearable cleanliness and hygiene.

I woke at 4:30 each morning, ate breakfast, and pulled on my running gear. I pocketed a cheap transistor radio for entertainment and information—this was way before the Sony Walkman, iPods, or decades before the first iPhone.

I then ran twelve miles into town. And what a run it was.

I ran along the edge of one of the country's five Great Lakes through residential areas lined with mansions.

I ran past sections of town that made me glad I was packing a gun in my fanny pack.

I ran through a downtown bustling with early-morning delivery trucks and past sleepy security guards, all-night diners, and hotel workers.

Finally, I reached my destination, a large, multistoried federal center in the city's heart. My usual arrival time was around 6:45 a.m., well before most of my office mates.

While many of these co-workers were very curious about my running routine, the more cynical ones didn't expect me to stick it out.

"Sure, it's fine while the weather's nice, but you'll never make it through the winter here," said one skeptic, summarizing what many others predicted.

My logistical and running system worked, although I was one tired hombre. Still, life was good. I loved my job; my young daughter was becoming an incredible little person, saying things like "raccamoni" for macaroni and "mazagine" for magazine; my wife, Donna, had settled into our neighborhood, and we'd found a church we liked.

Without us noticing, summer turned into fall and fall into winter. Meanwhile, I kept running to work. As the morning temperatures reached new lows, the cynics would stop by my desk when they arrived at the office.

"You run in today?"

"Yep."

When the temperature dropped to twenty degrees, they'd ask, "Run in today?"

"Yep. Brisk but nice." *Grrrrr.* I could hear them grinding their teeth.

The temperature dropped to ten degrees.

"You didn't run in today!"

"Yep, cold. But the lake—wow, beautiful."

Then the first mega-blizzard hit.

When I started running to work that morning, the temperature shot from ten degrees to a balmy thirty degrees. By comparison, I felt like I was in the Bahamas.

As I ran and listened to music on the radio, a news anchor broke in and said we were in the direct path of a real doozy of a storm. By then, I was halfway to work. As the wind blew the snow sideways, it was like a movie shoot where the Director ordered, "Snow and blizzard winds," and then the film crew turned on giant fans.

What kept me from turning around was a sub-sonic, fifty-mile-an-hour tailwind at my back. Each airborne stride took me about five extra yards; I felt like superman at the North Pole. A fifty-mile-an-hour tailwind, I reasoned, was a hell of a lot better than a fifty-mile-an-hour headwind. So I stuck with it and ended up at work twenty minutes early.

When I got in, I was covered with icicles and snow and looked like Nanook of the North. By then, the city was in an emergency, and no one else could reach the office. As a result, the night crew was ordered to stay put until, and if, relief could arrive. That left the poor night supervisory agent to deal with the phones that rang off the hook.

I volunteered to help field the flood of calls, including many from agents who were unable to make it in. Here's a typical call.

"Who's this?"

"Steve Gladis"

"How'd you get there?"

"I ran."

"Bullshit."

"No bullshit."

"Bull...shit"

We'd go back and forth a few times. Some flat-out didn't believe me. I'm guessing they thought it all a sleight of hand, a magic trick of sorts—or maybe I lived downtown under the building.

One of the hundreds of calls we got that day was from a newfound media friend who, unlike me, had been a distinguished collegiate runner. He'd been assigned to write a weather story about the blizzard. So, he called various agencies and businesses to see how each had handled the weather.

This reporter knew I had been running to work to train for the Boston Marathon and thought I was nuts. But as a runner himself, he regarded me as a quirky kind of nut. Here's generally how our phone conversation went.

Reporter: "Hey, you made it in?"

"Yep."

"How'd you get in?"

"Ran."

"No way."

"Uh-huh."

"Bullshit."

"No bullshit."

"Bull...shit!"

After settling down, he asked me more pointed questions to get to the truth, which he figured I was hiding. I recognized the interrogative technique but had all the answers and never wavered because it was true—I *had* run in, almost flown in. His intense interest showed me that the story of my snow trek had turned into THE weather story of the day.

The following day, the reporter sent a photographer to catch a candid shot of me running on a snow-covered street near our downtown office building. That afternoon, the local newspaper published a long, embarrassing photograph of me on its front page and a story detailing the eccentric commuting habits of "The Running FBI Agent."

From that point on, for better or worse, especially among ball-busting agents, I was called "The Rabbit." But the newspaper story had a bright side. With the end of winter drawing near, I had finally silenced the doubters. No one questioned anymore whether I had run to work.

10

Crazy Cases

My oddball ways continued as I ran long distances and chased bank robbers. After the blizzard, people regarded me somewhere between a rock star and an alien—neither label I wanted.

At one point, I took a values assessment developed at the University of Pennsylvania to identify my strengths. The results showed that my top value strength was "creativity," which probably would have been dead last on the lists for most FBI agents.

This creative streak—and a perspective that seemed one hundred eighty degrees out of sync with my agent colleagues—put me in a position to have some unique experiences during my time at the Bureau. Here are a few especially memorable cases.

Creative Bait Catches a Big Fish

The oxygen of any successful FBI agent is the criminal informant. Starting in new agents training, we're taught that informants solve cases—and they do. Cultivating informants, however, is a lot like raising kids. Both require much work that's ultimately worthwhile if you don't weaken along the way.

As an extroverted guy, I found informants entertaining and relatively easy to cultivate. Thus, my stash of informants was extensive and varied. Hookers, bartenders, bus drivers, neighbors, and a random person walking down the street where I was hunting for a bad guy were all fair game as informants.

On one occasion, an agent on our squad was hunting for "Orca," a guy nicknamed after the famed killer whale at the San Diego Zoo in the 1960s. Orca was massive, about six feet five and around three hundred pounds. He had been involved in murder and assorted other aggravated felonies.

We'd gotten information from a neighboring field office that Orca was heading to our town, and we had a few ideas on where he might stay for a night or two. An informant called the case agent to let him know he'd just talked to Orca and gave the telephone number to the agent. Because we wanted to arrest Orca physically, we tried to match the phone with a street number. The phone number turned out as we suspected: unlisted.

It was 5 p.m. on a Friday when most offices began to shut down for the weekend. Of course, we were deep into this Orca thing. But we also knew that federal judges and magistrates—whose authority we would need to subpoena documents from the telephone company for its unlisted records—would be unavailable during the weekend.

That night, we called our friends at the telephone company. The few on weekend emergency duty just laughed at our request to obtain subscriber information for an unlisted number without a subpoena.

So, as the clock ticked and our lead got older and colder, agents began to manually pour through files, trying to locate any reference to our newly obtained phone number. Watching these agents was like watching a bunch of bean counters trying to find a pinhead of a needle in a haystack the size of Pittsburg.

It came to me just after I called Donna to tell her it would be a long night. "Listen, I have an idea," I told the assembled group.

Whenever I utter the words "I have an idea" to a colleague who has worked with me for more than a day or two, the response is almost universal: "Oh boy! Here we go again."

"Hear me out," I said, marveling at the fib I was about to unleash. I then suggested pretexting: calling and pretending to be someone else to get the necessary information. "I've done this before," I told the group.

Technically, I was telling the truth. In high school, I used pretexting to find out about girls I wanted to date, see if they were home, and avoid fathers. I'd changed my voice by muffling it into a towel and filled my mouth with candy, sounding remotely like Marlon Brando in *The Godfather*. So yes—I *had* done pretexting before, though not the kind I was about to propose.

When we were chasing Orca, it was during an era when local radio shows often held contests to encourage audience participation. The contests all used the same formula: the disc jockey asked listeners to identify a mystery sound, an actor in a movie, or some product associated with a music jingle in exchange for a chance to win a prize.

Thus, the big idea came to me. I blurted it out as much as a brainstorm as in desperation.

"I'll call the number on a radio contest pretext to get him to give up the address."

A couple of guys waved me off, but no one protested. With no more thought than that, I ripped the phone from its cradle, dialed the number, and waited as my pulse began to rise in my throat.

"Yeah," said a deep voice, sounding as if it belonged to a big man or one with a chronic throat allergy.

"Hello, this is Josh Blackstone from WKWK, the city's best hot rock station," I said. "Sir, congratulations! You've been chosen to win a free case of Campbell Soup if you can sing the first couple of lines of the Campbell's Soup Song."

No sound came from the other end. I figured Orca was thinking, and that was dangerous. I jumped in. "Remember, it starts, M'm! M'm! Good…"

"Yeah, M'm! M'm! Good," he said, with enough energy to suggest that the big guy actually knew the song and, what's more, truly wanted the soup.

"Good start, sir. M'm! M'm! Good. That's what Campbell's Soup is, M'm, M'm..."

"M'm! M'm! Good," he blurted in deep, whale-like sounds.

By now, I had an audience of several disbelieving agents who'd gathered around my desk.

"Congratulations," I said, then burst out with, "Sir, you are a winner! Now, if you just stay on the line, I'll put you on with one of our staffers, who'll take your soup order."

I clicked the hold button and watched Orca blink for about three seconds. Then I picked up the line and said in my best staffer voice, "Hello, sir, this is Sam. Which kind of Campbell Soup would you like? We have Chicken and Rice, Chicken Gumbo, and Cream of Tomato." That was all I could think of on the spot. I racked my brain to visualize my wife's pantry, but I could only come up with three soup types.

Nothing. *Shit, he hung up,* I thought.

"Sir?" Nothing. "Sir."

"Yeah."

"Chicken and Rice, Chicken Gumbo, or Cream of Tomato?"

"What?" Orca was likely in and out of a drug stupor.

"Soup, sir."

"F— if I care."

"Okay, sir, we'll send you a mixed case."

I knew I had to close the deal fast because Orca was fading fast. "Sir, I need your address to deliver the soup in the next hour."

"Huh?"

"Anyone there who could help us with the address?"

A giggling woman, who undoubtedly had never heard Orca sing, grabbed the phone. I explained the contest that Orca had won, and she gave me the address.

About thirty minutes later, we arrived and joined the local cops who quietly surrounded the place. We raided the apartment, waking up Orca and Giggles. On the way out, I whispered in Orca's ear, "M'm! M'm! Good."

Case Closed.

The 75-Year-Old Extortionist

One day, while driving around searching for bank robbers on the city streets, I got another "payoff" from signing up for language school. "Signal 12345 (not my actual credential number)," the car radio crackled. "Please landline the office immediately."

"Roger that," I said, pulling over at a store to call on a pay phone (some may recall this ancient device).

The dispatcher directed me to a large city about thirty miles away, where a person of interest was accused of extortion. He spoke no English but did speak the Eastern European language I supposedly learned at language school.

Since it had been several years since my foreign language training, I was beyond rusty and could barely say "hello" in this language. Until now, I had been able to hide my language incompetence by relying on another agent in our field office, a near-native speaker, when a crisis required a translator.

Unfortunately for me, the agent was out of town that day. My luck had run out.

Realizing my incompetence, I swung by my house to pick up a translation dictionary. Then I headed to my destination, praying that the bad guy had the decency to help me fake a good translation.

I arrived at the address, expecting to find a seamy, broken-down house that looked occupied by a criminal. Instead, I saw a yellow cottage with a rose garden on the side, shrubs along the front, and a neatly trimmed lawn.

When a fellow agent opened the door, I saw his partner seated in a living room with furnishings you'd expect your grandparents to have—an old mahogany, clunky television console with water stains, a couple of well-worn upholstered chairs with a paisley pattern, an old fake oriental rug, walls decorated with artwork from a department store.

Seated on a couch covered in clear plastic sat a second FBI agent. He stared vacantly in the direction of a seventy-five-year-old man who snored melodically in an oversized, upholstered chair.

After introducing myself quietly so I wouldn't awaken the gentleman, I asked, "Where's the suspect?"

The agent on the couch pointed toward the elderly man.

"What?" I said loud enough to stir Rip Van Winkle but not fully wake him. "What's going on?" I asked more quietly.

"This old guy threatened to burn down his neighbor's house if the neighbor didn't keep his dog out of the guy's front yard. The two neighbors have been feuding for years."

"And the FBI is now involved in dog disputes?"

"Rip Van Winkle here used the telephone to make good on his threat, and the neighbor finally got tired of his bullshit and called the cops, who promptly punted 'the case'[he used air quotes] to us because of the extortionate telephone call—the interstate aspect. Bullshit but technically correct."

"Extortion? This guy?"

"Yeah, I know."

"Does he speak any English?"

"Nope, except 'bastard' and 'gottdam.'"

Ah, I thought. *We at least have some linguistic common ground.*

"Great. Okay, let's wake him up."

The other agent aroused the gaunt old guy, whose face looked more like a shriveled prune caricature than the gruesome kisser of a hard-nose extortionist. He rustled, grunted, and then said something in his native language.

A thought popped into my head: *If I could get rid of the other two agents, they wouldn't figure out how incompetent I was in the older man's language.*

So, I said, "I'd like to be alone with the suspect. Based on my experience with people from his country, he's more likely to talk one-on-one." I ad-libbed as I went along, sounding so logical that I began to believe myself.

The agent sitting on the plastic-coated couch didn't need any prodding. Within seconds, he and his buddy bolted for a smoke break near the rose garden, leaving me alone with the alleged extortionist.

"Namen?" I asked, not consulting my dictionary.

He looked at me like I was from Mars.

"Name, Nam?"

"Ah," he said, recognizing vaguely that I wanted to know his name. "Claus Von Stubbin."

"Gut."

He smiled, then the flood gates opened. For about two minutes, he spewed a barrage of machine-gun-fast language. Despite my protestations to slow down ("Nein schnell, Bitte, bitte! Nein schnell!"), Claus hurled words at me like he was putting out a three-alarm-fire with a five-inch-wide fire hose.

I let him spray until I couldn't take it anymore, then said in a loud, stern voice, "Halt, nein, halt!" or something along those lines. He clammed up and almost saluted.

Now I was faced with the prospect of having to lead the discussion. So I just stared at him. My mind spun fast but got nowhere, like rear tires in the mud.

Finally, I developed a couple of weak possibilities. Option one: pretend I had instant laryngitis and use homemade sign language. Option two: fake being a native speaker would expose my inability to translate and suggest I could not resolve the situation.

I chose option one. I coughed a few times, said, "Gottdam," and then pointed to his neighbor's house and the phone. I then pointed to him, shook my head "no," and squeaked out a raspy, "Nein, nein, nein!" Then I ran a finger under my throat in a cut-throat manner and pointed at him.

His narrowing eyes fixed on me like a rabbit in the crosshairs. He got every word of it. But to make sure and because I was on a roll, I did my pantomime again. In my best sign language, I told Claus to lay off the phone and the neighbor, or I'd come back and hang his ass from the closest tree.

He put his hands together like he was praying (because he was). I signaled for him to stay put and then went outside to join my two colleagues, who were having a smoke and talking sports.

I explained in a semi-intellectual, purposely confusing way that the old guy promised never to call his neighbor again. I explained that these old Eastern European guys kept their word, especially when talking to someone they thought might be a fellow countryman—even a sign-language, muted countryman.

I also added the obvious: we had better things to do than haul a seventy-five-year-old curmudgeon into a federal court over a dog pissing on his roses. They agreed and went back to talking about sports. I then called the U.S. Attorney, who only stopped laughing long enough to agree not to persecute Claus.

Case closed.

The Hot Dogs

Most FBI agents have a love-hate relationship with the press. They love it when the press helps them solve cases and hate it when the press criticizes them. The FBI public information officer, who serves as the media liaison, is seldom credited when the news coverage is good—but held accountable when it isn't.

As the media liaison for our field office, I constantly searched for human interest stories about FBI employees, especially agents. Whenever I got even a whiff of a positive story, I stiffened up like an Irish setter.

One night, I sat at my desk, reading the paper—an occupational requirement for any media guy. Usually, I looked for things that could hurt the FBI or its cases, but ninety-nine out of a hundred times, I just caught up on who was screwing whom in local government—the usual stuff.

On this particular night, I heard a couple of agents talking and laughing as they rounded the corner to where my desk was located. As they walked past, I smelled smoke. Because many agents have an affinity for barbecued or smoke-cured food, I didn't think much about it when they tossed their jackets on a chair, sat down, and started eating the sandwiches they'd toted in, still joking with each other.

It might have been my innate curiosity, the overpowering smell of smoke, or their laughter, but something attracted me to these two hyenas. I headed in their direction.

"Hey, what's up?"

They laughed and ate.

Remember that most agents saw the media guy as both agent and part-time pariah, a kind of Rodney Dangerfield agent who got zero respect. Sitting in a vacant chair and putting my feet up demonstrated that I was willing to wait for these two guffawing diners.

Finally, they finished their food. Then one guy turns to me and says, "Okay, Okay. We're driving down the street back to the office. We spot this building smoking. We call it in. Then we spot an old lady hanging out a second-story window. We tell her to get out. She keeps yelling something. So we yank her out before the place goes up like a bonfire. She starts screaming about her goddamn dogs. She tells us to save them. Like idiots, we go back in for them—a couple of mutts. One nearly bites us. The fire truck gets there, and we get the hell out. The smartest thing we did all day."

These two guys told me a story they would likely title: *Dumb Woman Lures FBI Agents to Near Death over Scroungy Mutts.*

Meanwhile, I heard a different story: *Brave FBI Agents Save Poor Woman and Her Dogs.*

When I told them my story title, they thought I was crazy. But after a half hour of explaining the positive PR angle, my two smoky superheroes agreed to the idea I wanted to pitch to the media. They left me alone in the office to start making calls.

My experience in the job taught me not to call the most prominent media outlet first; instead, to start with small weekly papers. They appreciated being considered necessary, and, most importantly, I got to practice my story pitch.

After a few calls to the weeklies, I called the local network affiliates and the important daily papers. Here's how the pitch went:

> Today two FBI agents while out on assignment [*forget that they might have been looking for a cheap place to grab lunch*] passed a building consumed in a raging fire [*okay ... so it was only a bit smoky at first—where there's smoke, there's fire*].
>
> Without regard for their safety, the agents stopped immediately and escorted an elderly woman from the raging inferno [*at that point, only a healthy barbeque fire*]. After ascertaining from the woman [*a ranting lunatic*] that her two dogs were trapped in the fire, these two heroic agents re-entered the inferno [*at this point an accurate description of the house in flames, which makes the two agents even more stupid*] and saved the two puppies [*mangy mutts who nipped at them the entire three flights down to safety*].
>
> The FBI is pleased to report that the woman [*dumber than a box of rocks*] and her dogs [*worthy of instant euthanasia*] are well due to these two heroic agents.

The next day, a major daily paper ran a front-page picture of the burning building with a caption that, in effect, read: *FBI Agents*

Save Woman and her Dogs. The agent in charge of our field office faxed the story to FBI Headquarters. The humane society called to give the two agents an award.

As for the two agents, they poo-pooed and made fun of the whole thing. Later, I caught one of them stuffing about ten copies of the paper into the lower right-hand draw of his desk.

Case closed.

The Nut Box

One of the less enjoyable agent duties in a field office is fielding telephone complaints from citizens. Often, we refer the calls to the local police, the sanitation department, or a psychiatric hospital.

Out of all the shifts, most agents view the night shift as the absolute worst for two reasons. One, it interrupts personal time; two, the alpha nuts come out to play when the sun goes down. We kept the names of regular callers—or the frequent flyers, as we dubbed them —in an index-card box labeled "Nut Box."

Being a misfit agent who saw things differently, I liked night duty as much for the change as for the host of characters I met on the phone. Here's what happened one night.

"Hello, FBI. Can I help you?" I answered as I took a sip of the worst coffee that a vending machine could make.

"This the FBI?" asked a man.

"Indeed, sir, this is the FBI," I said, "May I get your name, sir?"

"I am The Clipper," the voice said without hesitancy.

"Okay, Mr. Clipper, what's your first name?"

"That's my codename."

Suspicious that The Clipper was a frequent flyer, I looked for his name through the index cards in the "Nut Box." Sure enough, there it was.

Hmm, I thought. "Okay, Clipper, this line is now secure. What do you have to report?"

His voice was slow and methodical. "The Russians have invaded me. They came one night while I was sleeping and drilled holes in my teeth, where my fillings used to be, and put in electronic transmitters."

"Sure, we can help you. Can you stop by the office at 11 a.m. tomorrow?"

As you can imagine, the FBI got more than its share of calls from people who heard voices and attributed them to the Russians. To help these folks quiet the internal voices, some of our more inventive agents devised a clever treatment: "grounding."

To implement this so-called remedy, I instructed The Clipper to bring rubber boots, a belt, and a box of paper clips. The next day, at precisely 11 a.m., the elevator bell dinged, and a little man wearing a black overcoat and a baseball hat walked out. He carried a brown shopping bag.

"Hi, sir," I said, approaching him and introducing myself. "Glad you could make it. Shall we go into a private room so that we can talk?"

"Yes, of course. I brought the boots, clips, and belt—just like you told me to do," the man said as he removed his hat to reveal a shock of wispy hair.

When we sat down, I asked him, "Now, sir, can you tell me about the problem you've been having with Russian radio transmissions into your teeth?"

He told me it had all started ten years ago when he slept one night. Two Russian spies snuck into his apartment. He was in bed and could not move because, he suspected, the Russians had injected him with some drugs. One spy, a big guy, strapped down The Clipper. The other, a little guy with glasses, put a large, opener-type object in his mouth and started drilling. The Clipper yelled, but nothing came out. The little guy drilled four back teeth and put tiny transmitters into them.

Straight-faced, I asked, "How did you know they were transmitters?"

"Because when they left, I could hear the Russian transmissions coming from the teeth they drilled, and it has been driving me crazy ever since," the man responded.

By now, I felt sad for this fellow and wondered if I'd mistakenly asked him to come in. *What I'm about to do is pretty bizarre*, I thought. *But maybe I can help him feel better.*

"Well, Clipper, we dealt with a case just like yours not too long ago," I said. "Another man was the victim of an illegal personal invasion, or an 'IPI,' as we call it."

"Yes, sir, we've seen this before and have figured out a straightforward, practical way of neutralizing your illegal personal invasion. Are you following me so far?" I asked, thinking about what I'd do or say next.

The man nodded his head and said, "Yes, perfectly."

"Now, sir, do you have the paper clips and the belt?" I asked earnestly.

"Yes, here," he said as he pulled a small box of paperclips from the bag and put them on the table. Then he opened his coat and showed his belt to me.

"Great," I said, grabbing the opened box and linking the clips. "Sir, I'm making a ground conductor to neutralize the electronic implants."

After some idle chat, I constructed a paperclip chain about five feet long.

"Okay, step one. We attach this ground to your belt. The ground must go directly from your belt and touch the floor," I instructed while making the paperclip string loop around The Clipper's belt in the back, just above his buttocks. The string dangled down his leg, where it hit the floor with an extra foot or so on the ground.

"Perfect, now for step two. Please put on your boots. They are rubber, are they not?" I asked, giving this step a more official tone.

"Yes," he said as he took the boots out of the shopping bag and pulled them, one by one, over his shoes.

"Fine, now for step three—the walk," I said. For the first day, I instructed, he would need to keep both feet on the ground as much as possible when walking. When he walked—for the first day only—he was to shuffle and not take natural steps because if he lost too much contact with the floor, the electrical ground would get broken.

"Now, if you are sitting or sleeping, keep the boots on for one day to ensure that the electrical ground maintains contact with the floor. Do you understand?" I asked.

"Yes."

"Okay, let's practice the walk. I'll demonstrate," I said, standing up. Then I shuffled my feet like I was practicing cross-country skiing without skis. The Clipper was transfixed as if he were receiving life-saving instructions before a commando raid into enemy territory.

"Now, sir, you try it."

"Okay," he said, standing and steadying himself on the back of the chair. He took one step, then another. Soon, he was shuffling around the interview room like a pro. Keeping a straight face was brutal at this point, so I faked coughing several times.

"Sir, I think you have it." After a day, the signal will lessen measurably, I told him. And every time it comes back, re-apply this remedy—rubber boots and paper-clip ground wire. "Eventually, it will go away permanently," I added confidently.

"Thank you," he said with happy eyes.

"Why, of course, let's get you on your way," I said.

After he had shuffled to the elevator, with his paperclip chain dragging behind him, he turned around and gave me a thumbs-up. Then he shuffled onto the elevator, ensuring his paperclip chain was fully onboard before the doors shut.

Case closed.

Art Au Naturel

Late one morning, my field office's Special Agent in Charge (SAC) got a call from a senior resident agent in charge of one of the outlying resident agencies—smaller satellite offices set geographically apart but connected to large regional FBI field offices. An agent in this resident agency had recovered a rental van with a load of artwork. The artist, contacted in Israel, said the art was stolen and worth millions. Assuming most artists inflated the value of their creations, the agent called a local expert, who surprisingly confirmed the art's high value.

After I caught wind of the recovery from the SAC's secretary, I suggested that the agent bring in the cache of artwork to our building's basement and that we issue a press release about stolen international art. The crook, who had grabbed the rental van at a rest stop, was a low-level thief, not Thomas Crown or some other worldwide-known man of mystery. But we did have an international artist and a lot of stolen art worth a boatload of money. I went with those basic facts and called everyone I knew in the media.

When the artwork arrived, we moved a dozen cars out of the garage and unloaded the most prominent pieces of sculpture outside of the Hershorne in DC I'd ever seen. Modern art isn't my cup of tea, but I still admired the bronze and plaster figures with wistful slopes and natural lines (little did I know just how au naturel they were).

Our underground garage was transformed into an art studio when we finished the task. Some figures were seven- or eight-feet tall; others could be held in your hand.

Before creating our makeshift studio, I had distributed a press release about the recovered art and called all the TV, print, and wire services to ensure they'd gotten the news. I also guaranteed unlimited access for four hours; then, the art would be shipped to its owner after being photographed and cataloged for evidence.

Since it was a slow news week, anyone with a camera bit on the release. An endless stream of photographers and TV camera operators captured the art collection from top to bottom.

The SAC wasn't in that day, so the Assistant Special Agent in Charge (ASAC) agreed to pose with the art. All he had to do was repeat a few words from the press release, stand near or hold a piece of art, and be photographed by a phalanx of media. The ASAC, a pleasant Friar Tuck-looking guy with a wicked sense of humor, hammed it up like he was in a high school play.

We laughed as he posed, pouted, and pointed at those massive art pieces arranged against a white wall as if they were in a police lineup. As news crews came and went, the ASAC kept posing with the same item: a triangular piece of art with fine lines feathered from a central indentation framed by layers of folds. While holding this object d'art, he sported the grin of a man who enjoyed his assignment—way more than he should.

At the end of the four hours, I thanked the remaining news crews and reporters, ushered them out, and wished them well. When I returned to the garage, and the ASAC saw me, he laughed almost uncontrollably. I just thought he'd had a great time, so I joined him. When he could catch his breath, he said, "That was unbelievable."

"Yep, great press."

"Yeah, that too."

"Huh?"

He picked up the triangular bronze object that had become his favorite piece.

"You see this?"

"Yeah."

"Look at it."

I did and said, "Okay?"

"Now, look at it very closely."

"Okay, so what?"

"It's a vagina … a bronze vagina."

"What?" I said as I inspected the piece more closely. "Holy shit," I exclaimed, responding to the ASAC's analysis of the bronze, triangular, and highly accurate physiological rendering of the feminine anatomy.

Within two days, the image of our grinning ASAC holding a bronze vagina in his hands appeared on every television network and in many newspapers across the globe—due to the photo's international flavor. Fortunately, the details of the bronze statue were sufficiently obscured by the wily ASAC's meaty hands.

Case closed.

The Misfit Field Agent—Key Takeaways

Tolerate weird routines. My running routine to train for the Boston Marathon was my form of mental therapy. Yes, it earned me a dubious nickname (The Rabbit). Still, it took place in the early morning, before my coworkers arrived at the office. Go with a weird routine if it makes your employee more productive and doesn't disrupt others.

Reward creativity that gets good results. The reward doesn't have to be financial (although it's nice when this happens). Often, it's enough to recognize and thank people for their unusual ideas and contributions.

Hear people out. You may decide an oddball's seemingly ridiculous idea is brilliant. At first, the hot dog-eating agents thought I was crazy when I suggested pitching a media story about their rescue of two scroungy mutts and their owner. Eventually, they agreed, and the pitch earned us some great press.

The Misfit Headquarters Agent

11

Next Stop: FBI Headquarters

To garner support for our field division, the agent in charge of my office sent a string of my press clippings to headquarters. Back then, a group of folks in public affairs kept track, by field office, of any stories, interviews, press conferences, and other initiatives that generated positive publicity (or "earned media," as today's PR mavens call it).

According to the rankings of comparably-sized offices, our field office led the others in almost every category. This discovery drew the interest of the powers in Washington and got me transferred to headquarters.

Next stop, the nation's capital: Land of the free, home of the brave, and epicenter of one of the worst commuting areas on this planet.

Each year, headquarters brings in scores of young, promising, and relatively independent field agents who have been doing what you might expect agents to do: hunting down and arresting criminals. When these agents come to Washington, things change radically for them.

A bureaucratic finishing school of sorts, the FBI's headquarters has a system not unlike that of the Pentagon, which provides a torturous career development path from junior-level combat commander, to coffee fetcher, to Colonel.

In the FBI's system, the field agents who come to headquarters start as coffee fetchers for chiefs of units. Then they return to the field as supervisors, return to headquarters as coffee fetchers for section chiefs, return to the field as assistant agents in charge, return to headquarters for more coffee duties, and finally become special agents in charge of field divisions.

The sad part was that, after a year or so, you truly believed the party line: headquarters rounds out an emerging leader's experience. From what I saw, headquarters *reduced* a leader's perspective—and sharpened your head to the point that allowed a dunce's hat to fit. Instead of experiences that widened their views, most agents had narrow tasks that weren't nearly as interesting or useful as the ones they got in the field.

However, I got lucky. And in the FBI—like most large and sprawling bureaucracies—being lucky is much better than being smart.

My headquarters assignment was in the Office of Public Affairs, which handled public relations and coordinated the FBI's public image. As part of that mission, we tried to show that the FBI was made of ordinary people who put their bullet-proof vests on one arm at a time.

The best part of this assignment was that I saw a lot of the FBI's inner workings as I brought in film crews to interview a wide range of specialists—from the laboratory technicians who talked about the science of criminology, to the case agents who discussed cases and the investigative process, to the FBI Academy instructors who explained how the Bureau trained its agents and police officers at the academy.

Commuting to work in Washington was no picnic. I lived nearly fifteen miles from my office and—no matter how much I wanted to run to work again—couldn't endure more than a half-marathon a day. So, I decided to commute by bicycle.

Each day, I pedaled back and forth to D.C. on my new form of transportation and learned, mainly, how to change flat tires. It wasn't until the last day of my first week of bicycle commuting that I learned the most critical lesson: bike brakes don't work well when it rains.

It rained hard that day as I sloshed home through puddles, high winds, and death-defying traffic. When I hit an inviting downhill less than two miles from my house, I put the pedal to the medal, or more accurately, put my foot to the pedal.

Traffic had been backed up, stop and go. When I saw the light turn green, not more than fifty yards ahead, I pumped my legs faster, wanting to get home as soon as possible to shed my soaking-wet running suit and shoes.

As I gathered a renewed head of steam, the light turned red. I hit the brakes.

Nothing happened.

Without even the slightest delay, I whizzed through—well, almost through—the intersection. Apparently, the traffic light was broken and flashed at irregular intervals, only allowing a few cars through at a time. This frustrating situation resulted, not surprisingly, in drivers gunning through the intersection when it turned green for a second or two.

I realized all this in the split second before I saw the massive grill of a car, which was not two or three feet from my right leg by then. The car hit me at an almost perfect right angle.

My bike skidded under the driver's front tires. I proceeded to tumble up his hood and onto his windshield until he stopped abruptly. I then tumbled back down his window, onto his hood, and did a five-point landing on the pavement.

I ended up smack in the middle of several lanes of traffic that mercifully stopped inches from my body. Though I could not feel my legs, I knew I was alive.

Thankfully, my injuries were not mortal—but I stayed home for several days to recuperate from a four-inch gash to my lower leg. In the emergency room, the doctor said I was lucky, which he didn't need to tell me since I was painfully aware of this fact.

After he left, I breathed a sigh of relief as I lay on the gurney. Then a state trooper walked in and handed me a failure-to-maintain-control ticket.

Welcome to Washington, I thought.

12

A Whacky Office at the Watergate

After I limped back to work and explained how I got my bike injury to my colleagues, they didn't know what to make of me. Most of them already thought I was an oddball based on their stories about me running to work in a foot of snow. Now the bike incident sealed the deal. In their eyes, I was a bonafide screwball.

Subsequently, I joined an agent carpool to get to work. Donna put her foot down and made me promise to cease the bike commute—or else. I didn't want to discover what "or else" meant, especially since we were planning our future.

Before coming to Washington, Donna and I decided to expand our family. Given the ease and joy of conceiving our first child, we figured the second go-around would be just as effortless.

Not so.

Months of nonchalant lovemaking, months of reproductive determination, and then months of disappointment and frustration led us to a fertility clinic. Donna endured several procedures to ensure her plumbing worked correctly. Then it was my turn.

Once in Washington, I made an appointment with a fertility specialist whose office happened to be, of all places, in the Watergate building (an ironic location for an FBI agent, I know). Moreover, a small, quasi-historical plaque outside my new doctor's practice proclaimed that the office was in the exact place of the infamous Democratic party break-in that led to President Nixon's "I am not a crook" claims and, eventually, to his resignation.

As a new patient, I had to fill out an extensive medical history form that might take as long as my annual income tax return. Then I sat there, waiting my turn.

Nearby, a group of four or five people sat and read in chairs and couches positioned around a large, expensive coffee table laden with magazines like *Time, Newsweek, Glamour,* and *Forbes*. Based on their relaxed manner, I guessed they were regulars who, after many visits, knew the drill. They were all dressed in designer suits or dresses—and looked upper-middle class.

On the other hand, I wore a modest, heather-green, three-piece wool suit I had bought on sale before coming to D.C. Secretly underneath my suit jacket were handcuffs, a loaded revolver, and a leather bullet pouch.

After a while, a young nurse appeared with a clipboard and a wide-mouthed plastic container, about the size and shape of a one-pound coleslaw container you'd get at the deli. She smiled and motioned for me to come over. We stood only a few feet from the gaggle of well-dressed readers around the coffee table.

"Welcome," she said as if I were visiting a restaurant for the first time. Affable and professional, she smiled, collected my paperwork, handed me the container, and pointed to the restroom. "We'll just need a sample."

Unsure, I said as discreetly as I could, "Urine?"

"Sperm," she said distinctly.

I kept my eyes away from the other patients, imagining them snickering at my rookie error. Without asking any follow-up questions, I sped toward the refuge of a small, unisex restroom located not more than eight feet from the coffee table.

Once in the bathroom, I noticed it had been thoughtfully, if not scientifically, equipped for the mission at hand—so to speak. On the back of the standard white commode sat copies of *Playboy* and *Penthouse*. Next to these magazines were a tube of lubrication jelly and a box of latex gloves, which I eyed dubiously.

Latex gloves, I thought. *Who in God's name uses them for this particular assignment?*

I looked at the magazines, the lubrication jelly, and the wide-mouthed, capped cup in my left hand. After placing the cup next to the *Penthouse* issue, I removed my jacket and hung it on the back of the door.

Next, I removed my revolver, broke it open to prevent accidental discharge, and laid it on the floor on tissue paper. I removed the handcuffs wedged under my belt in the small of my back and put them on another tissue next to the revolver. Then, I pulled down my pants and sat on the toilet.

With my vest and tie still on, I realized that things could get in the way, so I took off the vest and waddled—pants-around-ankles—to the door, hung up the vest, and shuffled back. I tucked my tie into my shirt like I was eating Italian spaghetti with sauce that might splatter.

This would be my inaugural—and only time—masturbating in a suit and tie. Given the office's rich political history, I hoped no one was videotaping me.

Next, I had to decide: glove or no glove, lube or au natural. I desperately wanted to try the glove and lubricant as a new experience but feared that changing horses in mid-stream was not a good idea. As my old coach had warned, don't ever wear new shoes in a game that matters. So, I chose au natural: ungloved and un-lubricated.

The next choice: *Playboy* or *Penthouse.* I'd always preferred *Penthouse* for its spotlights on certain anatomical parts. But as I sat in my suit (technically, half a suit), not much was happening, especially since the tiny bathroom was next to a handful of chatting people who knew precisely what I was up to.

I leafed frantically through *Penthouse* and found my sure-fire, erection-worthy helper: The Penthouse Forum.

I've always gravitated to this section, which has stories like the one about a young guy who hitchhikes a ride with a gorgeous, love-starved older woman. She asks the young man if he minds removing her clothes after they allegedly pull off the road to get a hamburger. And while I am fully aware that pulp fiction writers probably authored these stories, I fell for them every time.

Boing!

Mission accomplished, I washed and dressed, once again concealing all my FBI gear. Then I walked past the smiling group of patients to the desk, where I put my sample in the nurse's gloved hand.

Thus began my fertility clinic saga. Thousands of dollars and many months later, I reached the end of my patience with a process that involved pokes, prods, exams, loose-fitting underwear, and a love-making timetable that rivaled the Amtrak Acela train's daily schedule.

One morning, at the height of my frustration, Donna suggested another procedure she'd just read about. I slammed my hand on the table and said, "No. No more. I've had it."

She looked at me dismayed but said nothing, hoping it would all pass. I read her look and said, "I mean it—no more. I've had it. I've whacked off so often at the fertility clinic that now whenever I walk by a medical building, I get an erection!"

A few months later, Donna got pregnant after I returned to wearing jockey shorts. It was a happy time. And now we could laugh at the stimulating memories made at Watergate.

13

The Shark Pen

Every summer, at the beginning of beach season, PBS, National Geographic, Animal Planet, the Discovery Channel, and other television networks and channels produce stories about sharks to scare the pants off us all.

The action scenes are always the same: a piece of not-so-prime beef is tossed overboard into seemingly calm, azure-blue water, and then—out of nowhere—about one thousand sharks appear, and a violent feeding frenzy erupts as the great white sharks smash and bully away the smaller sharks to get to the meat.

Picture this scene, and you have nature's equivalent of the FBI's career development process.

In due time, Donna and I welcomed our second daughter. At work, I learned to navigate around headquarters—a place that was (and I suspect still is) survival of the fittest or, at a minimum, survival of the fiercest.

Not everyone could grab the brass ring—the next promotion on the FBI's career development pyramid. From its broad base of field agents, the pyramid narrowed to a stiletto-tipped point of special agents in charge, senior headquarters executives, and of course, the capo dei capi, the megalodon of sharks—the FBI Director.

I liked most of my supervisors, some not so much. Since I had many bosses at headquarters, I'll aggregate them into one effigy: "Roland."

Roland, a savvy guy who had learned how to survive on the scraps of meat tossed to him by senior executives, had seen agents like me come and go for decades. Over time, he'd become a shark referee in the career development shark pen.

In addition to Roland, I worked with many smaller sharks, most of whom were trying to do a good job, punch a career-development ticket, and move on to their next promotion. While swimming in this pool, you inevitably met great whites who knocked aside the naïve sharks (like me) to kiss Roland's ass.

To do this, the FBI great whites watched the smaller sharks swim cautiously toward Roland with some offers—maybe a tidbit of helpful information or a hard-fought accomplishment that made the executive look good (and thus, enhanced the standing of the small shark). Then at the last second, just as a smaller shark was about to pay homage to the executive, a great white swooped in and snatched the offering from the lesser shark—who may have naively revealed his offering in advance while asking for the great white's advice.

This kind of mugging happened to me several times. One great white, "Archibald," also tended to report my doings and unconventional views. If I voiced a criticism, he gave a blow-by-blow account to Roland, damaging my prospects for advancement and enhancing his own. Indeed, Archibald subscribed to a self-serving philosophy: to make his candle burn brighter, he had to blow out all the others around him.

My enthusiasm has always been my greatest asset—and my most significant liability. Many years later, I now understand how I must have appeared despite my best intentions to make things work better, if not more creatively. Therein lay the rub that rubbed some folks at FBI Headquarters the wrong way.

One day, this tendency reared its head when a field Special Agent in Charge (SAC) did a TV interview on a national network. Roland summoned several of us to watch the video of the SAC as he was grilled by a well-coiffed, smart-ass reporter, who, no doubt, was a great white in his pool.

The interview took about ten minutes and involved a case I can't remember. But it was on national TV, so it must have been significant.

I remember the SAC, who was maybe in his late fifties. He looked like he'd been up all night, perhaps a few nights (which is common in major cases). And while he wasn't Mr. Sunshine or some great orator like Cicero, I thought he did a decent job.

After we had watched the video, Roland began the discussion.

"I think the SAC looked nervous, even defensive."

When the Greatest White Shark leads off with that comment, you can probably guess what old ass-kissing Archibald said.

"Me too."

The roomful of sharks followed suit. "Yeah, he seemed annoyed about having to answer the questions." "I agree; look at the way he scowled." "His answers seemed curt, almost flippant."

The idle, self-serving tut-tutting continued as Roland listened and nodded, fueling the feeding frenzy. Then I spoke.

"I don't agree."

All the other sharks swiveled and stared at me. Exorcist-style, Roland pivoted his head in my direction and asked, "How so?"

Like the village idiot—or, in this case, the village shark—I thought we were there to tell the truth. So, I proceeded with my assessment.

"I guess that the SAC had been up all night. And what's more, that reporter is a national guy, who we all know is a real jerk."

There's no way that I could have known that Roland liked this reporter on a personal level. But like many agents at headquarters for a long time, Roland had established deep relationships with certain reporters. Unbeknownst to me, one of those relationships developed with the reporter I'd just called a jerk.

Roland's face reddened. Unfortunately, I didn't read into it— and kept digging my hole deeper by defending the SAC.

"Yeah, so the SAC's up all night under tremendous pressure, and old numb-nuts barges in demanding a story at three in the morning. The only thing I can see wrong was that the SAC agreed to talk to that jerk."

You could call my blunder a self-inflicted wound to my career. You could call it utterly naïve. You could call it stupid beyond all comprehension.

And you'd be right on all three accounts.

The discussion ended abruptly. As most of us left the room, Roland stopped Archibald and pulled him aside for a private conversation.

Within a month, I was transferred to the FBI Academy, a move that would double the time of my already hellacious commute to work. My new job would be managing the academy's public affairs office.

Effectively, Roland banished me from headquarters as a form of punishment. But the intent of his actions—and my new assignment—wouldn't pan out the way he had hoped.

14

Back to La-La Land

Although I had spent time in Quantico before, it wasn't until my second stint that I realized the FBI Academy was the Bureau's equivalent of Siberia. Located over fifty miles from headquarters, the academy was an island of broken toys and rejects. Many of us were offbeat, like your crazy uncle or aunt whom the family talked about at holiday gatherings.

We'd all been tossed down here by the big sharks because we didn't fit in anywhere else and thus were viewed as dissidents, enemies of the state. By putting us all in a separate, far-away location, the big sharks reasoned, we could less corrupt the rest of the shark population.

As the academy's public affairs officer, I worked directly for the assistant director of the academy's training division. My primary responsibility entailed fielding media requests to visit and film around the academy.

And by far, the most popular spot was Hogan's Alley, the academy's tactical training facility.

Designed by Hollywood set designers, Hogan's Alley had the look and feel of a studio lot at Universal Studios. It consisted of an entire town with a post office, a bank, and a hotel, among many other buildings. This simulated town aimed to create a realistic environment where agents could receive hands-on training to deal with situations they might encounter on the job.

Visiting media crews loved Hogan's Alley, whose Disney-like effect grabbed them like kids getting on the "It's a Small World" boat ride. Journalists watched as agents repelled off high buildings, hip-shot at the expansive ranges in unison, and handcuffed each other. This activity generated hundreds of photo ops and bedazzled even the crustiest reporters, who quietly fantasized about being secret agents.

We strategically gave FBI hats and T-shirts to everyone on the media crews—camera operators, sound engineers, and reporters. This practice taught me a good lesson: when building friendly relationships with the media, never underestimate the power of free trinkets with the letters "FBI" emblazoned on them.

On the Hogan's Alley "studio lot," many agent instructors revealed themselves as frustrated actors. The instructors did their shtick before their classes and received critical feedback at the end of the semester—thumbs up or down in student evaluations.

For the instructors, these evaluations were just as critical as the reviews of an actor after opening night. Generally, those agent instructors who improved stayed at the academy—those who didn't left with their tails between their legs.

Most agent instructors fell into two categories: regular, more traditional agents and misfit agents. The typical agent, "Harold," ended up in a two-year assignment at the academy because of some quirk in the career board selection process. Harold subscribed to the same tedious teaching method his high school math teacher, his (or her) college chemistry professor, and drill instructor in the Army used. When he taught, Harold talked, and people pretended to listen.

Harold's teaching style bombed with the harsh, veteran police officers and FBI agents who were his students. Having no sense of good instruction, Harold bore down even harder and—as evidenced by his students' evaluations—failed twice as fast. The result: Harold was out the door as soon as he fulfilled his two-year assignment at the academy.

Then there were the misfit agent instructors who, like me, ended up at the academy because they were "different." These instructors did not fit well in the field or at headquarters. But they tended to be natural actors, entertainers, and teachers. From my observations, many nontraditional agent instructors also knew how to get the best out of their students. Their preferred teaching method was a dialog in the classroom, not a monolog from the instructor.

* * *

Despite being "dumped" at the academy, I decided to enjoy myself until my time was up and then move on to a field assignment. I still suffered from the illusion that I could learn to be like other FBI agents.

I still hadn't figured out where I belonged at that point in my career. Yet somehow (through osmosis, perhaps), the academy's misfit agent instructors had left a mark on me—and planted a seed for a new path that would reveal itself before too long.

15

A Silver Lining

During my two-year stretch in the academy's public affairs office, I found outlets for my creative streak and my unconventional view of the world. One example was a newsletter I dubbed "The ComPost," a takeoff of The Washington Post. The newsletter was a hit among the academy's more conservative members, who viewed our local newspaper as not much better than birdcage liner.

I also began teaching occasional classes to help some misfit agent instructors when they were out sick or traveling. Before long, I parlayed my substitute teaching experience and the scraps of knowledge I had acquired about handling the news media into a new class that became part of the academy's curriculum.

In my class, I taught strategies to deal with the media during hostage situations. It was a subject I knew well from my field agent days when I had been involved with several hostage-taking cases that attracted national media coverage. Most of my students were senior-level agents and officers since they would likely need this type of training in their field leadership jobs.

I illustrated key lessons with vivid stories about some of my past cases, such as the serial bank robber who was caught in a bank with a dozen captives and the jilted boyfriend who kept his ex-girlfriend hostage until she dropped her two kids out the window into the waiting hands of (thank God) a deft agent. I later learned that this photo was nominated for a Pulitzer Prize.

Here are three of my more tongue-in-cheek lessons:

First, many people show up when a guy with a rifle and combat gear enters a prominent company's building and holds hostage a gaggle of buttoned-down, pin-striped executives. Half the people root for the hostage taker, the other half for the snipers. Nobody roots for the guys in the pin-striped suits.

Second, journalists multiply like rabbits. The longer the suspect holds the hostages, the further away the media travels. Also, the ever-expanding media crowd must be regularly fed information, if only to tell them the types of sandwiches delivered to the hostages for lunch.

Third, every police officer within three thousand miles—and a handful of cop wannabes with badges they got in pawn shops—show up to help. Usually, the "help" consists of standing around drinking coffee, eating every donut available, making fun of the FBI, discussing local sports, discussing national sports, finding the nearest bathroom, and calling their families to tell them they'll be home as soon as they solve the case.

Over time, I refined my lecture, making it more entertaining as I shared helpful tactics. Along the way, I discovered that I loved the classroom.

Let me be clear: I did not go willingly to the FBI Academy. But looking back, I now realize the great whites at FBI headquarters did me a huge favor that changed my life. Essentially, I'd been fired into my passion.

Despite my newfound affinity for teaching, I didn't pursue it immediately—partly because I resented my assignment's mandatory nature. My natural ambition to go as far as possible in my chosen profession also propelled me.

My next move would be decided by the FBI's Career Board, which was little known to the outside world—but wielded tremendous power within the FBI organization.

16

A Fateful Pee Break

The FBI Career Board, which made decisions about supervisor transfer assignments, was comprised of a dozen senior executives. Each major division within headquarters had a representative on the career board to ensure that all transfer candidates, no matter how qualified (or unqualified, for that matter), got a shot at fairness.

Any transfer candidate with an iota of political savvy figured out a way to get someone on the board to champion their cause. Some agents in the queue for a transfer did better than others, depending upon the power of their division representatives.

As my assignment in the academy's public affairs office neared the end, I took no chances. I buttonholed three career board members for whom I had worked. Fortunately, all three were still willing to talk to me.

The career board system allowed all transfer candidates to select three desired field offices and rank them in the order of preference. Naturally, I wanted an assignment that would advance my career. But I also wanted to stay in the Washington, D.C. area for both family and financial reasons. Thus, I lobbied for a promotion without the transfer.

I tracked the activities of the career board like investment bankers track the Dow Jones. Based on several well-placed friends, I knew the exact day, time, and phase of the moon that my case would be heard.

On that fateful day, I got word that I'd be staying in the Washington area and had been assigned to a local criminal counter-terrorism squad. Naturally, I was ecstatic that months of lobbying, groveling, and whining had yielded such a beneficial personal dividend.

The reality was that I was unqualified to run a counter-terrorism squad at the time—knowing less about terrorism than I did about origami or taxidermy. While feeling guilty and underprepared, I figured that if I first subscribed to the old Hippocratic Oath, the do-no-harm rule, I could serve my selfish needs, those of the FBI, and the nation.

But what gave me pause was the haphazard nature of the negotiations, whose outcome changed the course of my life.

As I mentioned, I had three career-board insiders working on my transfer.

"Mr. One," with whom I had worked for several years, now served as the agent in charge of a nearby but out-of-town office.

"Mr. Two," also for whom I had worked in the past, was a strong supporter of me and the agent in charge of another non-local office on my radar.

The third guy, "Mr. Three," was another supporter I had worked with.

Mr. Three had no dog in this career board fight because he was firmly entrenched at FBI headquarters and could not benefit from my transfer. That wasn't the case for Mr. One and Mr. Two, which I had not correctly calculated before the meeting.

Word has it that when my case came before the board, my name was favorably discussed for three field offices—one in town (my personal preference) and two that were good alternates but required a transfer. During the discussion, my career became a chrome ball in a pinball machine, banging off one electronic blinking rubber bank into another, hitting a flipper, and bouncing back into play in another direction and still another.

Self-interest, politics, inattention, and weariness played into marathon meetings steeped in emotion, exhaustion, and bladder-challenging sessions. Finally, it was a bio-break that saved my career.

According to insider reports, Mr. One and Mr. Two continued to bounce my career around. So Mr. Three, the no-dog-in-this-fight guy, decided it was time to regroup and called for a "bio-break."

Once in the bathroom, Messrs. One, Two, and Three were finally alone. As they all stood at parallel urinals, Mr. Three negotiated my future. He reiterated that my career preference was to stay in Washington. He also extracted a promise from both Mr. One and Two to put my professional well-being before their self-interests.

They agreed and zipped up. Hopefully, they also washed their hands, though that detail was not conveyed to me.

The Misfit Headquarters Agent—Key Takeaways

Assume good intent. My enthusiasm has always been my greatest asset—and my most significant liability. In hindsight, I now understand how I must have appeared despite my best intentions to make things work better, if not more creatively. If the misfits in your organization are rubbing people the wrong way, they're probably not doing it intentionally.

Listen to the message, not the tone. Misfits tend to have communication challenges. Many are overly introverted or extroverted (or blunt). You may learn something valuable if you ignore the noise and listen to their message.

Champion oddballs when they deserve your support. I landed a job promotion I wanted because I had three FBI career board members who stood up for me at a pivotal moment during a long, contentious discussion. Regarding the career paths of good team members who contribute to your organization, don't let quirkiness derail their progress. In the end, talent is talent, regardless of its wrapper.

The Misfit Field Supervisor

17

Newbies, Geriatrics, and Devoted Cynics

Located only an artillery shell away from FBI headquarters, my new field office was larger than most. It had a Special Agent in Charge (SAC) and several Assistant Agents in Charge (ASACs) who oversaw the front-line supervisory squad special agents (like me).

My tour of duty as a field supervisor began with a prophetic phone call on the first day I walked into my new office. Back then, the country of "Tabasco," as I'll call it, was both a hotspot and a political hot potato. That hot potato was about to land in my lap, as luck would have it.

When I answered the phone, the caller stated my name as if he was reading it from a list. "Get about a hundred agents and surround the Tabasco Embassy," he commanded.

The voice added, "Surround the Tabasco Embassy—there are four suspected terrorists inside."

I jotted the instructions after scrambling to find a scrap of paper in my new, utterly cleaned-out desk. As the man was about to hang up, I said, "Okay, I'll talk to the agent in charge and advise him. But where the hell is the Tabasco Embassy?"

That question symbolized the zero-base of knowledge I had about diplomacy or terrorism. Yet for the next four days, I commanded—with several more experienced supervisors and an ASAC—a siege of the Tabasco Embassy.

During that period, discussions took place between Tabasco's ambassador and various State Department and FBI negotiators to release the four terrorists to the FBI. Assuming these radicals all had diplomatic immunity, the best we could do was deport them once they were in custody.

Time seemed to move at a snail's pace as the siege continued. The fatigue of living in a car for four days, with only brief periods when we could go home for rest, began to wear on us all.

At one point, a tweed-suited and cuff-linked U.S. diplomat arrived at the embassy and demanded to speak to the Tabasco ambassador. Having lost much of my patience, I told him it wasn't a good idea, given that four terrorists may be lurking inside. I also explained that we had snipers trained on the building's door and window.

He stiffened, showed me some papers, and managed to get to the ASAC, who told me to let him through. As he passed by, I asked the diplomat one parting question.

"While talking to these guys at the door, could you move either to your right or left so our snipers get a clearer shot at the terrorists?"

He stared at me, shook his head, walked up to the door, and knocked on it as if he were selling magazine subscriptions. The door cracked open, and the face of an older man appeared. The State guy handed the older gentleman some official-looking papers and left.

That was that. Later, the terrorists agreed to leave the embassy and the country. The siege was over.

Thus began my new assignment—and my wild ride as the field supervisor of the counter-terrorism squad.

Terrorism back then wasn't well understood, and what little there was to understand, I didn't know. Thankfully, I had my squad—a weird combination of action-oriented SWAT types and contemplative thinkers tempered by older, gotten-their-asses-kicked guys. All of these squad members, in their way, helped me through my steep learning curve.

Soon after the Tabasco embassy incident, a former government official from the country of "Garlic" was assassinated in the U.S. by a militant group after he spoke out against the regime in his former country, and the dictator of Garlic decided to have him whacked.

Our squad responded with vigor and determination, given the volatile relationship between the U.S. and the country of Garlic—a relationship that still stinks to this day. Almost overnight, the counter-terrorism squad doubled to about fifty agents, bigger than some FBI field offices.

I quickly assigned an assistant supervisor, "Mike," to run a particular sub-group investigating the assassination. Mike was the hardest-working, most determined agent in the office. Sometimes he was rough around the edges and saw no need to smile or coddle anyone. But he knew his stuff, had an intensely analytical mind, and was generally calm.

Mike took over the ragtag sub-group of odd birds and whipped them into shape. I acted as the chairman of the board, and he served as the CEO. Together, we managed this special spinoff squad with the intensity of an emergency room at a city hospital.

All agents gathered twice a day, at 8:30 a.m. and 4:30 p.m., for briefings in which each person reported what he had accomplished that day—a level of accountability that few had ever experienced, except those who'd been in combat, like me. The new agents loved the briefings; the older ones hated them. But we did them every day for well over a year.

We also organized this F-Troop of agents into "clusters" of four or five agents, with a mix of experienced agents and new agents in each cluster. The new agents brought an energy that stimulated the older ones to get going and cover leads, and the more senior agents brought wisdom that kept the new ones from doing anything too stupid. It was symbiosis in action, with the younger and older agents complimenting each other like peanut butter and jelly.

Ultimately, Mike and this squad of strange bedfellows unraveled a sophisticated assassination plot that implicated the hierarchy of the country of Garlic. Along the way, they discovered a gang of U.S. citizen supporters—ex-strong-arm robbers and other criminal types—planning to carry out similar assassinations around the U.S.

As one older agent said, these terrorist supporters were, "Just a bunch of assholes looking for a place to be assholes." We escorted many of them back to a place they knew well: jail.

18

A Bomber Threatens a D.C. Landmark

After solving one of the most complex terrorism cases at the time, Mike received a prestigious law enforcement award and was heralded as a terrific friend of local law enforcement. By then, I had separated my squad from the special sub-squad that investigated the assassination, and Mike was a newly anointed field supervisor for the latter group.

All in all, Mike was in a good place—until our field office got a new ASAC with a reputation for being a jerk. Like many new sheriffs in town, the ASAC wanted to prove a point and pee on rocks to mark his territory. Unfortunately, Mike was the first rock he peed on.

The new ASAC was argumentative and hostile when anyone in the office raised terrorism issues. Then one day, the poop hit the proverbial fan.

I was returning from a meeting when the car radio crackled with news about a man threatening to blow up himself and a Washington landmark in the city's center.

The bomber, dressed like Sergeant York (the celebrated American hero of World War I), had a large backpack and an electronic switch in his hand. The backpack, he claimed, contained a massive pack of dynamite.

The first rule of hostage negotiation is to start communicating with the hostage taker as soon as possible to calm him down. By the time I arrived at the landmark, an hour had passed—and no one had talked to this guy. He was getting more agitated with each passing minute. Not the best start to a negotiation.

I met with the cops and agents who were already on the scene, and because I was a trained negotiator, I elected to chat with Sergeant York, though first praying that my life insurance policy was paid and up to date.

About that time, a detective from another agency rolled up to what he considered *his* crime scene, not uncommon in an urban area where there were more law enforcement agencies than languages in the world, and each agency claimed primary jurisdiction over the other. In this urban forest, everybody heard it and claimed the wood if a tree fell.

"Detective Krumpky" reminded me that he also had jurisdiction and would accompany me to chat with Sergeant York. I agreed to take him along—after he had removed his sidearm, a condition stipulated by Sergeant York.

Krumpky and I approached Sergeant York with extreme caution. When we got within fifty feet of the bomber, he told us to stop, take off our jackets, and turn around.

As we did, Sergeant York noticed a pair of handcuffs behind Krumpky's back. The detective had undoubtedly forgotten about the handcuffs hooked onto his belt.

Big mistake, though understandable.

Sergeant York erupted and told us to get the hell out of his territory. We stalled but hustled out of his presence when he reached for the switch.

Hundreds of people—including the SAC, the new ASAC, SWAT team members, local police, and cops from about fifteen other agencies—had shown up by now. The news media arrived in droves. After a while, it looked like a Hollywood set.

I decided to stick with my role as a negotiator because none of the usual negotiators from our office had shown up yet. I relayed my decision to the powers that be and moved on.

Krumpky—who felt this decision was his to make, not mine—wasn't happy. In hindsight, I should have picked up on his displeasure, which he somehow transmitted up my chain of command. Before long, I got a call from the SAC to report to the command post set up some distance away.

By then, our usual negotiator had arrived, and he and Krumpky wanted me out of the scene. I protested to no avail. The SAC insisted I stay at the command post and relinquish the negotiations to the other negotiator now that he had finally shown up.

19

Blowing Up My Career

The next day, the atmosphere at the field office was tenser than usual. I felt a tropical storm brewing. I also sensed that I was in the eye of the storm but wasn't sure why.

Then the new ASAC called me into his office. Detective Krumpky, he said, had complained about me. Our field office's relationship with Krumpky's law enforcement agency was in jeopardy.

I felt the winds of the storm picking up.

A week or so later, I was called into the SAC's office and told that an internal investigation was underway to determine whether I had damaged a critical relationship. In the meantime, I'd been relieved from my role as the supervisor of the counter-terrorism squad.

I was stunned and hurt—not to mention angry. I argued but got a stone face and a reiteration of my fate.

The first problem I faced was breaking the news to my squad. I tried to take the high road and made some excuses about the process working its way through, and as a temporary measure, it was best for me to step aside until the facts were in. All the time, I knew, as did they, this was my swan song.

My next problem was finding an office since I was now a supervisor without a portfolio. Ironically, the much-lauded special squad I had helped create to investigate the assassination had taken the last space available on our floor.

I wandered about for a day or two looking for office space, with no one helping me or standing too close to me. When you're "under a cloud," as they say in the Bureau, your friends are too busy to join you for a cup of coffee or lunch. You learn to connect with your inner self and perhaps one courageous soul, usually another "broken wing."

Mike was that courageous soul. He and I went to lunch or had coffee nearly every day. During those days, I learned a lot about humanity and humility. I will have respect for Mike for the rest of my life.

Finally, I found a place to set up my office after another business moved out of the building, leaving the entire floor below the main office vacant.

When I went to look at the space, I found a mess of discarded equipment, hanging loose wires, and dirty rugs littered with plaster that had fallen from the walls. It had all the charm of a football locker room after everyone had showered and left without tossing away the used tape wraps and wet towels.

Welcome to my new Siberia, I thought. *My new home in exile.*

After I cleaned up the space, I transferred my old office furniture and set my desk in front of an impressive bank of windows that probably was coveted in the previous office arrangement. When my desk, lamps, chairs, and couch were all arranged, it looked like a Hollywood set in the middle of a vast warehouse.

When anyone accidentally stumbled onto the floor and found my little oasis, they were both impressed and amused. I'd hear, "Man, you have enough room?" or "Hey, nice neighborhood."

The humor helped. I often greeted people by saying, "Welcome to Siberia," to beat them to the punch.

Still, I had nothing to do, which killed me more than the ostracism. I worked out at the gym as much as possible to stay in shape and prepare for my next assignment, which didn't seem forthcoming.

Weeks later, the SAC called me and told me that the internal investigation found I had hurt relationships with Krumpky's agency. My assignment as supervisor of the counter-terrorism squad was officially over.

"Now what?" I asked.

The SAC shrugged his shoulders. Headquarters hadn't determined what was next for me.

Back to the gym?

20

Fighting the System

One of the guys in the gym, "Bartholomew," was a highly placed assistant to the FBI director. He worked on special projects, most often legal issues. An intellectual in an organization that eschewed them, Bartholomew was a fellow misfit. I suspect that, earlier in his career, he, too, had felt the sting of banishment.

At any rate, Bartholomew took pity on me and knew I could write. He called the SAC and got me assigned back to headquarters to work for him.

Talk about a deus ex machina! I had been plucked from a desert island and brought into the king's palace, the Director's office.

In my new role, I worked like a maniac, in early and home late. The long days almost felt like heaven after the cruel sentence of isolation and no work assignments for weeks. And there I stayed, working for Bartholomew—for whom I'll be eternally thankful.

Though I acquired many new, nerdy headquarters friends who joined me for coffee or a sandwich without fear of retribution, Mike and I still went to lunch. One day, he mentioned that the new ASAC at the field office was starting to work on him—documenting every meeting, calling Mike in for the slightest issue with a case, dropping by for surprise mini-inspections, pulling files and going through them with a fine-toothed comb.

But it wasn't until Mike received an unsatisfactory rating on his annual performance assessment that he knew the ASAC planned to shed him.

Mike told me that he would fight his trumped-up evaluation. By then, the new ASAC had also completed my evaluation. Though it wasn't at the level of my past "outstanding" ratings, it wasn't something you'd typically protest—especially given my new ad hoc assignment.

So there I was, sitting pretty at headquarters and working for a decent, intelligent, non-malicious guy. When I learned that the new ASAC had decided to remove Mike, I came nose-to-nose with a professional dilemma.

Should I sympathize with my friend, rail at the idiot ASAC, and then return to my safe, quiet office at headquarters, do nothing, and just take my gentleman's above-average B rating?

Or should I step up and take on the system with my buddy, the guy who stood by me through the worst part of my career while saving a lot of Americans from the scourge of terrorism?

I want to say it was an easy choice and that upon my return to the office, I drafted a stern letter of support for my colleague and former subordinate. Well, I didn't. I waited, weighed, and chatted with my friends and with Donna. I contemplated the matter like I was a president deciding whether or not to go to war.

It's hard to remember the catalyst that prompted me to appeal my rating in support of Mike, but I think it came after I had offered the ASAC a thick packet of my accomplishments. I also submitted a detailed memo in support of Mike's performance.

The ASAC said he thought my rating was decent and that—in general—he thought performance ratings had become overly inflated.

I replied that I agreed with his point but morally had to protest. He disagreed and said the rating would go to headquarters, where I could register my complaint and request a third-party review. And that's precisely what I did.

A few days after my protest, I was told I had unceremoniously transferred back to the field office. My pleasant respite was over.

What assignment would I receive? Where was the hotspot that demanded my sudden presence back in the field office from where I had been gone for months—only to be exhumed after I decided to mess with the system?

I was transferred to oversee (drumroll, please): The FBI Applicant Squad.

Widely regarded as the proving ground for newly minted supervisors, the applicant squad was one of those thankless squads designed with fatal flaws. Its mission was to conduct detailed background investigations of FBI applicants, federal judges, justice department employees, and White House appointees, among other applicants from various agencies.

Supervisors were destined to fail because of the crazy rules and staffing policies that kept the applicant files backed up on the file shelves. The applicant squad intended to show veteran supervisors how bad their assignments could be, especially if they screwed up like me.

Welcome to my new world of predetermined failure.

An FBI Academy instructor's advice to new agents resurfaced in my mind. *Sharks eat fish who swim funny ... don't swim funny!* By deciding to protest my appraisal, I had swum funny. My shark ASAC responded by transferring me to an assignment that guaranteed a bad outcome.

The first thing I did was call for an all-squad-agents meeting in my office. They probably expected a let's-all-do-a-good-job speech from the new supervisor. The new agents from Quantico were the first to show up; the deserted, abused, older, cynical agents staggered in ten minutes late, five minutes before me.

I huffed in and shut the door, cramming ten pounds of people into a tight, hot, five-pound bag. Irreverently, I explained the ASAC had a contract out on my career—I was a dead man walking, just waiting for the firing squad.

My honesty stunned even the most cynical agents, who started to pay attention. As far as I saw, if any of them screwed up, I'd take the heat because it didn't matter—you can't kill a dead man. It was like being on death row and getting a library fine.

I explained they could do a great job, and I'd go to bat for them in ways that would make them proud. I was already prepared to argue for several older agents and rattled off their names, much to their shock and surprise.

The results were unpredictable, shocking, and nothing short of remarkable. The agents left the office, all but high-fiving themselves and me. I got firm handshakes, especially from the older guys I'd planned to recommend releasing from administrative bondage.

Within a month, productivity statistics for the squad had hit levels rarely before seen. However, my non-plan of acting like a dead man worked by chance. Before long, people were reluctant to leave. And those who did go sang the praises of a supervisor who cared but was mildly suicidal.

After I had settled in on career-death row, I learned about a possible opening at a unit within the FBI Academy. I knew the head of the unit, "Stanley," and made a trip down to Quantico to talk with him. During our meeting, I explained with excruciating honesty the bounty on my head and the risk involved in bringing me into the fold. It was like I'd thrown a piece of meat in front of a hungry German Shepherd.

Stanley, an "alpha misfit leader," snapped up the bait. Within the month, I was transferred from death row to my form of heaven: teaching.

The Misfit Field Supervisor— Key Takeaways

Leverage oddballs' strengths to get the best out of others—and vice versa. Pair misfits with partners who will grow and benefit from the oddball's creativity, a different perspective, and unique solutions to problems. When managed well, strange bedfellows can produce remarkable results.

Know the difference between power and authority. Power gives you the capacity to exert your will over someone else. Authority gives you the formal right to make decisions and issue commands. Most misfits don't do well under autocratic leaders who assert strong authority and expect unquestioning compliance and obedience from subordinates. Keep this in mind when assigning people to teams.

Learn people's backstories. An oddball's behavior will make more sense when you take the time to listen to their personal stories. You'll better understand why they do what they do.

The Not-So-Misfit Academy Instructor

21

Back to La-La Land Again

At the FBI Academy, I was an old dog sniffing a familiar hydrant that smelled like roses. The freedom of thought, the peaceful atmosphere, the arching pines, the winding roads—paradise compared to the nuthouse I'd just left.

For the first time in months, I could think without worrying about someone trying to assassinate me or at least seriously wounding my career. One morning, as my mind whirred during a run, I thought of an analogy that helped me understand my uneasy fit with the counter-terrorism field office—and with the FBI in general.

The agents in FBI field offices are like a construction crew that builds a home. Brick by brick, these agents carefully and systematically build cases—ensuring the right amount of spacing and daubs of mortar between each brick. Beam by beam, and board by board, they construct the structure, the floors, and then the walls of tall, broad, and complex cases that, one day, will be subject to the jarring inspections of a judge, jury, and defense attorney.

Just as you'd want a top-notch bricklayer or carpenter to construct the house where you'll be living for years, you want a field office agent who uses a craftsman-like approach to gather detailed information from wiretaps, surveillance logs, fingerprints, hair and fibers analysis, handwriting exemplars, DNA, and other sources used to put serial murders, spies, terrorists, and white-collar crooks in prison.

Then there's me. I'm no craftsman, as my wife will tell you. She remembers, all too well, the bathroom leaks that became significant plumbing projects, the gas leaks that required emergency actions, and the ruined sports car engine, among the other disastrous results of my do-it-yourself repairs.

No, I'm not the guy you want trimming your doors or installing your window frames. I'm more like an architect who can step back, look at the big picture, and then tell you which overall design would work best for your custom-built home and where you should place it on your lot. I can't count the trees in the forest. But I know innately which forest we should harvest for the wood.

That bird's-eye perspective is the one I brought to FBI investigations. If you had to choose between a ten-thousand-foot worldview (like mine) or a ten-foot worldview held by most good field agents, I'd go with the field agents and hope that few high flyers walked in the door by mistake.

Fortunately for me, the academy housed flocks of ten-thousand footers. A halfway house for theorists, intuitive thinkers, and broad-brush painters, the offices and classrooms reverberated with a myriad of discussions about the Hersey-Blanchard Situational Leadership Model, Myers-Briggs personality types, Maslow's hierarchy of needs, and Leon Festinger's cognitive dissonance theory.

And because the FBI offered extensive free training through its FBI National Academy program for law enforcement personnel, there was no shortage of captive, well-fed, and on-the-federal-dole police officer students. So we had ample opportunity to sing the latest theoretical songs to audiences of ten-footers who usually responded, "Huh?"

Stanley, the supervisor who saved me from field office torture, was an alpha misfit ten-thousand-foot leader. Long in the theoretical tooth, he'd have been far better off writing novels or sailing around the globe. But I'm glad—and eternally grateful—that he didn't because he saved many a wayward soul—like me.

A modern Don Quixote, Stanley never saw a windmill where he could resist tilting. And he was good for countless laughs as he raged against the machine. We laughed until we cried—none more than "Edgar," my best friend at the academy, and me.

Throughout my life, I've always sought out level-headed, sane people to keep me from shooting myself in the foot. Edgar fit the bill perfectly. Edgar quickly became my confidant, friend, wise counsel, a guy with steady hands (even after a few brews), an eye for detail, a wicked sense of humor, and a passion for teaching.

We laughed and joked at the system, the students, the staff, and each other. It all made the academy immensely entertaining both in and outside the classroom.

The fun didn't stop there, however. Some of the characters I was about to encounter would make my assignment even more amusing.

22

Teaching Cops to Communicate

At the academy, I taught writing and public speaking classes as part of a leadership program for police officers. The cops were all rising stars in their respective departments. For them, graduation from this national program was a feather in their caps—and possibly a ticket punch toward a desired career as a chief of police.

The students came from departments that ranged in size from over thirty thousand officers to fewer than ten. So, you had cops from New York City and Mayberry R.F.D.-type towns in the same class, a mixture that made for some colorful academic tapestry.

Teaching cops to communicate equates roughly to teaching a Kodiak bear to dance. You hope to get an acceptable outcome and have fun but not get eaten alive.

In one class, I taught these street-wise-but-novice public speakers the importance of a strong introduction. To deliver a good speech, I explained, you needed to open with a grabber, an "attention getter." I gave examples of several techniques, including a startling statistic, a memorable quote, and a relevant story. Students took notes for their next assignment: a seven-minute informative speech that incorporated at least one technique for an effective introduction.

On the day of the presentations, I sat in the back row and took notes as the students gave their speeches. Some were excellent, most fair to middling. But I'll never forget the one delivered by "Kojak," a New Yorker.

After Kojak walked to the front of the classroom to deliver his speech, he hefted a large square object onto the podium. A dark cloth covered the thing, about the size of a two-foot squared box. I thought I heard something moving within, but I quickly attributed the sound to the rough way he had set down the box.

His speech was about criminal informants, the bane of a criminal investigator's existence. From my experience, they often committed crimes themselves or lied to please you or to help their case.

Knowing what I did about informants, I was interested in what Kojak had to say about them. I settled into my chair and waited expectantly.

Kojak stood barrel-chested in a tie-and-coat ensemble that looked like a purchase from a Goodwill store. Mismatched, tacky, and roughhewn, he cleared his throat and belted out in a robust New Yorkese:

"They're called informants, sources, assets, snitches. But in New York, we call them…"

He paused as he reached over and grabbed the dark cloth over the square object.

Then he repeated his lead-in.

"Like I said, in New York, we call them—RATS!"

He tore away the black cloth as he belted out the word RATS. Underneath was a wire cage that contained a scared and seemingly ravished rat about the size of a small dog or a full-sized fat cat.

The mega-rat snapped at the cage with its teeth and claws with such ferocity that the entire class let out a collective "whoop" and moved as far back in their seats as the molded plastic allowed.

"HOLY CRAP!" one guy yelled. That summarized our collective reaction to this speech opening.

My pen had been poised to circle a five on the one-to-five scale next to the "Attention Getter" category on my grade sheet—but I, too, jumped back, leaving a streak across the page.

Undoubtedly, this officer had grabbed—or maybe hijacked—our collective attention.

Kojak continued his colorful speech as the class members returned to their seats. He gave examples of New York cases that informants had broken. He also cited highly credible law enforcement statistics that generally would have impressed the hell out of me.

The problem was his speech introduction had been, well, too attention-grabbing. His audience was distracted by the mega-rat gnawing at the all-too-frail-looking cage that seemed to rock back and forth every time this demon from hell slammed against the cage. The saliva dripping from its teeth only heightened the anxiety levels of the assembled, now huddled masses.

Usually, I did not try to coach students as they delivered their speeches unless it was an emergency—say, for example, their fly was down. I decided this was one of those exceptions.

So, I motioned to Kojak to put the cover back on the cage. He misinterpreted my gestures and talked louder over the gnawing, spitting, and rattling of his "prop."

By now, fear had morphed into hysterical laughter as the speech had turned into an absolute side show—me waving my hands as I gagged on my gales of laughter; the audience members, many of whom had left their front row seats for higher ground who hooted and guffawed.

As all this was happening, Kojak tried to finish his speech and thus meet the course requirement.

And the rat? It kept gnawing and rocking, looking like it would eventually escape from its not-so-gilded cage.

Thank God it didn't.

23

Handling Drunks Who Don't Want to Go Home

The FBI Academy had a dining room called "The Taproom," which, in true Jekyll-and-Hyde fashion, transformed dramatically at 4:30 p.m. By day, it was a place where faculty and other staff lunched; by night, it was a bar where pitchers of cheap beer flowed and cops a long way from home, and under academic pressure, unleashed their underlying tension.

On any given evening, at the height of pro football season, around two hundred beefy, rowdy, and more-than-slightly inebriated cops gathered in The Taproom, talking, laughing, yelling, clapping, and booing at whatever game was on the TV monitor. By 11 p.m., The Taproom's closing time, the crowd was ripe. Just about everyone was drunk, loud, and a bit testy.

That's when the duty agent arrived.

Every FBI agent assigned to the academy had to be the duty agent three or four times a year. It was mostly a tedious assignment, where you were the glorified head of security who patrolled the halls at night and slept on a lumpy mattress in a dorm room. Of all the duty agent's responsibilities, the least fun—by far—was closing down The Taproom. This task required the skills of a hostage negotiator.

The first rule was never to get to The Taproom early—big rookie error. New duty agents showed up at 10:45 p.m. and tried to get a jump on clearing the tables by walking around and telling people it was last call. This usually resulted in more than a few "F— yous."

More seasoned FBI duty agents waited until around 11:15 to arrive. By then, all the lights blazed, and ninety percent of the customers had returned to their dorm rooms.

One time when I was the duty agent, the clock struck 11:15—and two tables of rowdies remained. Table number one had a bunch of FBI SWAT agents. Each guy in this group was the size of a pro football player. In their camouflaged garb, they looked like Klingons, the swarthy, ruthless humanoid warriors in *Star Trek*.

Table number two consisted of a half-dozen crusty cops who I normally could roust without too much trouble. Usually, I had to warn them, then get tough with, "Don't make this shitty job any worse for me by making me call your chiefs and get them outta bed. What do you say, folks?" That approach usually worked. Even drunk, most cops didn't want to go round on the phone with their chiefs.

This evening, however, would require some setup and deft handling, given the circumstances. So I began by baiting table number two.

"Okay, you guys, get out now," I said, knowing the reaction I'd get by throwing such a heavy gauntlet before a bunch of wasted police officers.

"F— you, man. We ain't going nowhere 'til we finish these pictures [sic]," one drunken galoot stammered as he pointed to three brimming pitchers of beer. "Okay," I said calmly, then walked away as they laughed. For drunk cops, the duty agent became an effigy of all FBI agents—I'm sure the beer pitcher guy called me "Wimp" or something equally as complimentary as I walked away.

Next, I wandered toward the table of FBI SWAT agents, who were seated behind a partition and out of sight of my new drunken cop "friends." I picked out the largest of the behemoths—a guy about six feet, five inches tall. With all his camouflaged stuff, he looked like one giant, mean hombre.

I sidled over to him and said, "Hey, I need some help. I got a bunch of belligerent drunk cops who won't leave and hate FBI agents. There are six of them and only one of me. You guys help?"

"Where?" was all he said. I pointed to table number two.

He motioned to his crew, who hardly knew what day it was. They assembled and marched to the table of cops, who were still nursing their pitchers.

When my new-found buddies encircled the table, casting a shadow on the cops, they looked up.

"Out," My Klingon friend said—a man of few words. The cop who had cast aspersions on the FBI said, "Screw you." I noticed he did not use the F-word again with my big new robotic friend.

At that point, the Klingon warrior reached down and pulled the cop to his feet. The Klingon, nearly getting on his knees to be nose-to-nose with the very fast sobering cop antagonist, said, "Now, asshole."

At that, the rest of the cops moved swiftly, indicative of good sense and miraculous alcoholic recovery. And as soon as the Klingon let the loudmouth down so his feet could touch the ground again, he too decided to leave with a faint, "Okay."

In the meantime, the barmaid had cleared the Klingons' table. So after the cops had left and the warriors headed back to their table, they saw it was empty. By now, all the lights were on, and the barmaid was jangling her keys at the door to lock up.

My new buddy looked down at me, the empty table, the barmaid, then back at me. He nodded, produced what might be called a smile, and said, "Okay."

As I watched him leave, I couldn't suppress a small smile of my own.

24

Fat, Dumb, and Happy

Teaching at the academy agreed with me—a good fit, as they say. And publishing was a part of that fit.

Every year, each instructor was supposed to publish an article, a white paper, or a lesson plan. For many instructors, other duties (like going on the road to teach police schools around the country) intervened. As a result, their intention to publish often went by the wayside.

But I took the mandate seriously. Before becoming an academy instructor, I started writing articles to express my views. My first published piece was about running to work for a well-known runners' magazine. From then on, I continued to write articles about running and fitness, primarily because such benign topics would pass muster with the FBI Headquarters reviewers who had to screen anything a Bureau employee wrote before it was published.

The mandate to publish academically oriented work opened a whole new writing territory. And I embraced it like a religion.

Rather than write many lesson plans that would only gather dust, I thought, *why not publish articles and compile them into books?* So that's what I did.

Article after article flowed from my pen (actually, my computer). I wrote feverishly, like a death row prisoner who wants to preserve his every thought, so his kids won't forget who he was. At one point, my reviewer and best friend, Edgar, observed, "I doubt that you've ever had an unpublished thought."

While it was said in jest, Edgar's comment wasn't off the mark by much. I wrote pieces on how to deliver a speech, how to use non-verbal communication, and why you should stick with simple language. How to answer questions from an audience and what you should and shouldn't do when handling the media in a hostage situation. Once the floodgates opened, I cranked out academic articles on other communication-related topics.

When I was writing, teaching, and brainstorming with fellow instructors, it was the happiest period of my life. As a Southern bard might say, I was fat, dumb, and happy.

And as is the Bureau way, the gods of career development would not leave me alone—mainly because I enjoyed what I was doing.

One day, I got a call from headquarters. A voice asked, "Would you like to write speeches for the Director?"

In the past, before my assignment to Quantico, I had applied twice for the position of chief speechwriter for the FBI director—mainly to escape other, less-desirable assignments. The application process required each job candidate to write a sample speech. Then a secret panel of three reviewers rated the speeches.

Having broken the circle of secrecy, I found out that, the second time, my speech received the highest rating. Still, I didn't get the job.

Each time I applied and wasn't selected, embarrassment accompanied the feeling of rejection. After coming up empty-handed two times, I'd had enough.

I'm fat, dumb, and happy, I thought. *Why not leave it alone?*

"Thanks, but no thanks," I told the voice on the phone.

A few days later, the same guy called again. "We'd like you to consider it—the job of chief of speechwriting for the Director."

Not many of my friends nor Donna thought the position was a great deal. But the lure of fame and fortune—plus the prospect of a few more bucks a week, a small office, and the challenge of writing speeches for a big kahuna who demanded excellence—kept gnawing at me.

"I don't think so, but let me give it some more thought," I said.

"Great. We're submitting your name to the career board for the position."

A week later, yet another call came in from the guy, whose voice was now familiar.

"Congratulations, you're it ... I mean, you've been promoted. See you in two weeks."

Panic would best describe the feeling I had inside—not unlike my reaction whenever I take on a new position. Exacerbating my terror was that the Director booted his last two speechwriters, and I was the final crack at recruiting an internal candidate for the job. If I didn't work out, the hiring people would go outside the FBI for a new chief writer.

Given this scenario, my fear of failure had some merit. Or, as Edgar used to say, "It ain't paranoia if they're out to get you."

Two weeks later, I entered the FBI Headquarters building and started my new job as the Director's chief speechwriter. My new office on the seventh floor, nicknamed Mahogany Row, was where the FBI's bigwigs worked.

I had closed the fat-dumb-and-happy door. And opened the scared-paranoid-and-very-serious door.

Hmm.

The Not-So-Misfit Academy Instructor—Key Takeaways

Don't jump to conclusions about misfits. Sometimes they're just on the wrong bus or in the wrong place. They transform and thrive when moved to a department that's a better cultural fit or when they're allowed to work independently.

Be open to unconventional solutions. Admittedly, my decision to bait two tables of drunk patrons against each other wasn't a neat and pretty solution to the problem of clearing out in the FBI Academy's bar at the end of the night. But it worked. And no one got hurt!

Consider the opportunity cost of job promotions. If I hadn't accepted the job as chief speechwriter for the Director, I might have stayed fat, dumb, and happy at the academy. On the other hand, I might have stunted my career advancement had I turned down the job. Opportunity cost is a significant consideration for your talented misfits. If the promotion doesn't work out, they typically have a limited selection of places to go within your organization.

The Misfit Chief Speechwriter

25

Working for The Man

I could have titled this chapter "FBI Directors I Have Known and Loved" (or, more accurately, known and respected) because I had worked for three directors. Rather than focus on any of the three, I'll aggregate them into one image: the Director.

To be successful, the Director needs a litany of qualities: an astute mind, a clear vision, incredible political instincts, experience running a vast enterprise, consummate executive skills, impeccable communication acumen, and a firm command of the law. Each director typically comes to the FBI's top office with only some of these attributes. The rest they acquire on the job, figuring out the tune as they hum along.

That's pretty much what I did after I became chief of speechwriting. In my role, I oversaw the FBI Speech Unit, which fell underneath the Office of Public Affairs. The other members of the Speech Unit consisted of one writer on his way out of the Bureau (the only writer the Director liked); another writer whose style wasn't the Director's cup of tea; a new, exceptional writer I brought with me from the academy; and the unit's secretary.

I didn't realize the depth of my challenges until I walked into my new office. One of the first things I tackled was the lack of technology. Back then, the Speech Unit had no computers except for the secretary's old, rickety word processor that only she knew how to operate. So I went where anyone at headquarters goes to find stuff:

the loading dock. That's where new items came in, and office furniture and supplies were "surplused" (a fancy word for tossed out).

I returned to the office, hauling a sizeable wooden dolly laden with six computers and screens attached to a gaggle of wires. We got the computers up and running in a couple of days, much to the surprise of my new staff and, frankly, to myself.

The writers in the FBI Speech Unit churned out speeches by the bucketful. Once onboard, I changed an essential part of the process. Before, the custom was to write speeches individually and put the speechwriter's name on the cover of the speech. I insisted on a group-editing effort, where we worked as a team and edited each other's speeches before submitting them anonymously to the gods in Public Affairs for review. That way, we would sink or swim as a unit, not individually.

At first, the writers balked at the change like Picasso might if he had to show his work to Van Gough before revealing it to the world and, to add insult to injury, unveil it without his signature. But none of us were Picassos, so we all sucked it up and submitted to the process.

Fortunately, this deviation from a long-entrenched procedure earned the support of my new boss—not a small thing, given that he and I started on tentative ground. When I first took the chief speechwriting job, he called me into his expansive and leathered office for a chat.

"When your name came before the career board, some people were concerned about how you handle stress," he said as he steepled his hands.

My mind whirred and hit on the D.C. bomber incident. *My old ASAC must have put a memo about the incident in my personnel file.* Given this ASAC's propensity for homemade psychoanalysis, it wouldn't surprise me if he wrote something like, "This guy's a stress bucket."

My new boss leaned back in his office chair.

"This is a stressful job you're taking on," he said. "But I think you can handle it. I had to speak up at the career board meeting and defend you."

Wait, speak up and *defend* me? I hadn't asked for this job. These headquarters guys recruited me as their last great hope before they had to go outside of the FBI for a hired-gun journalist. My new boss defended me because of a memo penned by a snake in the grass.

At first, I was stunned by his seemingly benevolent gesture. Then I became pissed.

"Stress, sir, is being a second lieutenant in the Marine Corps and being shot at every day. *That's* stress. This is just a challenging job."

He looked at me for a long moment. Then a broad, genuine smile spread across his face. This guy knew how to motivate people, as I learned that day.

As we stood up, he shook my hand and wished me luck. No doubt I was going to need it.

26

The Word Whores

Inside the FBI, the culture revered the Director as The King of the Bureau, the giver of all gifts, great and small. Externally, his public persona translated into "Santa and his elves." He was the jolly (okay, maybe "politically skilled" is a better descriptor) Saint Nick. The rest of us were his elves, helpers, and happy hands.

Out of all the Director's elves, the ones in the Speech Unit had to be the quietest. In effect, the speechwriters weren't just elves. We were more like what I'd call "word whores."

When the Director spoke in public, the media, Members of Congress—and sometimes the entire free world—scrutinized his every word. That's why he couldn't function without word whores. He needed us badly but didn't want that fact to be known. So, we would come around, perform our secret writing acts, pick up our checks, and then skulk off into the darkness.

As a result of this mindset, we were treated well but ignored. It was almost as if we didn't exist. We never received credit when a speech won kudos and made the Director look good. But we were held accountable if things went south for any reason.

I can count on one hand the number of times the speechwriters met with the Director to hear his view or ideas for an upcoming speech. Much of the communication gap was due to the Director's grueling schedule and introverted personality. He communicated solely through written notes, instructions relayed through personal assistants. He chose any method other than a direct conversation with the person writing the speech (God forbid he got caught associating with the word whores).

Our standard assignments consisted of speeches for law enforcement groups, civic organizations, associations, community groups, and chambers of commerce within major cities. Usually, the topics and venues were predictable. Occasionally, we got an oddball, exciting request.

The Director once agreed to present a retiring federal judge with a set of bookends—and needed a suitable quote for his talk. His office called in the morning and asked us to submit five or six possible quotes by the end of the day.

I turned this assignment into a contest with two writers to make it fun. We all agreed to toss a dollar or two into a kitty and research some quotes. We would bundle our recommendations and send them all to the Director. He had some favorite quotes and tended to stick with this list. But if he happened to choose one of ours, the contributor got to keep the money in the kitty (a whopping pool of less than five bucks).

After lunch, the two writers gave me their quotes. One was along the lines of "Knowledge will reveal the truth." I don't remember the other, but it sounded similar. *Pretty airy stuff,* I thought. But I submitted the recommendations anyway, on the off-chance that one of them might be added to the Director's list of favorites.

Later, we learned that—sure enough—the Director chose a favorite quote from Supreme Court Chief Justice Oliver Wendell Holmes. That's when my two writers confessed to me about their "research." Their quotes came from the fortune cookies they consumed when they ate lunch together at a Chinese restaurant. Neither writer won the money—but we all got a laugh out of their research technique.

As demonstrated by that incident, I never knew what might happen when these two speechwriters collaborated. I can't say enough good things about them, both of whom had their quirks. "Hanna," the writer I brought from Quantico, was an exceptional talent and became a more fantastic writer than expected. She also had a wicked sense of humor and little respect for incompetent authority figures—which worried me sometimes.

The other speechwriter, "Sam," was younger and had much less literary experience than Hanna or me. But he had potential because of his rabbit-quick wit and creative eye. Like many creatives, his writing initially required more structure and several revisions. Over time, he got pretty good—thanks partly to his artistic union with Hanna.

Along with Hanna and Sam, several other good writers came and went. We also had exceptional support staff, especially my executive assistant, "Anne."

Quiet, reserved, well-read, and self-assured, Anne was the ballast of the organization, spanning the previous speechwriting chief's and my tenure. She proofed all the speeches before they went to the head of Public Affairs and then to the Director. Anne's eagle eye saved us from many embarrassing moments. It was the intellectual equivalent of someone telling you about a piece of toilet paper stuck to your shoe.

I was conducting an editing session with the speechwriters in my office one day. We'd left the door open, which was unusual but fortuitous. I'd asked one speechwriter to read a section of his speech aloud so that we could hear the language.

After he finished, I heard a soft voice from outside my office, "the Director would never say that."

We all stopped talking, startled like we heard something go thump in the night.

"Anne, was that you?" I asked.

"Yes."

I asked her to step into my office to explain what she meant. She told us matter-of-factly that she'd transcribed hundreds of recordings of the Director's speeches. After five years of listening to the Director, she'd developed an "ear" for what he might or might not say.

From that day forward, we subjected all our speeches to "the Anne-Sniff-Test." If a particular sentence or passage smelled funny to Anne and struck her as something the Director would not say, that was that. We figured out another way to say it.

27
Networking in the Cafeteria

The frustration of being the Director's writing concubine was somewhat alleviated by a gymnasium in the basement of the headquarters building, whose architectural style was described as "New Brutalism" for its likeness to a massive Japanese bunker from World War II. The place looked like Frank Lloyd Wright designed it while he was on mind-altering drugs. Cantilevered slabs of concrete flew in every direction, creating a structure that could seemingly withstand a direct hit from a nuclear bomb, let alone some feeble terrorist attack.

Every morning, before the telephones could ring, before people could stop by to give me a copy of a great speech they'd just read in *Time* that I might be able to emulate, I worked out at the gym before the crack of dawn.

I ran until I nearly dropped to get a good dose of endorphins—free Prozac. After my workout, I stopped for a cup of coffee in the cafeteria, one of the Bureau's natural wonders.

A large, coliseum-size eating venue that serviced over seven thousand hungry employees, the cafeteria matched the pace and rhythm of its patrons. It opened its doors early enough for the insomniacs to get enough coffee to render them officially conscious.

The place became bustling in the summer when the Bureau hired the college-age kids of employees for security reasons (clearing their backgrounds took much less time) and financial ones (the summer jobs helped underpaid employees and their kids handle college tuition). My oldest daughter took advantage of this employment opportunity.

Each day, most folks at FBI Headquarters eventually found their way up to the cafeteria. Some people dashed into the cafeteria, grabbed their coffee, rolls, or whatever, and blasted back to their desks to tackle their work.

Other cafeteria-goers, like me, used this time to network with fellow inmates and to watch the rest of the world go by. Usually, smaller groups grabbed the square, four-top tables, and larger groups gravitated toward the round, six-top tables near the windows of full-length glass that looked out over the city.

The talk started with the obligatory pleasantries: "Hey," and "What's new?" and "How are you?" One morning, a conversation at a four-top went something like this.

"I heard Jack Sprat got the desk in Chicago—OC Desk (organized crime supervisory squad)."

"Yeah, and Smitty is on the list for Baltimore."

"Jesus, look at that."

The guy who uttered the last statement stared at a gorgeous young woman as she passed by the cashier and made her way to the condiments table to fix her coffee. All conversation ceased except for comments about the woman.

What happened next was sexist. Read to the end for the punch line.

"Who is she?"

"I don't know, but what a body."

As three of the table's occupants commented, the fourth remained quiet. The conversation continued.

"Man, I'd like to…"

Suddenly, the fourth guy leaped to his feet.

"That young woman happens to be my daughter. So, keep your goddamn remarks to yourself."

Silence for a few seconds.

"So, how about the Redskins this year?"

28

From Speechwriting to Publishing

The Neanderthals I encountered in the cafeteria didn't exactly enhance my time at headquarters. Neither did a work environment where I was often addressed as "Hey, you!" by people who reported directly to the Director.

Every speechwriter I've known burns out eventually. Being kept in a back room, at the beck and call of a public figure (who would deny you even exist), gets old. So does dealing with demanding assistants. Most of them couldn't write their way out of a paper bag, yet that doesn't stop them from telling you to "put a lawyer joke here "or "add a little more zip there."

After a couple of years of toiling in the Director's office, I'd had enough—and thought a jailbreak was the only way to go. So, I looked around for a slow boat to China and found it when a colleague in Public Affairs decided to retire. He seemed pleased that someone wanted to take over his job as the editor for two publications: *The Enforcer*, an external law enforcement journal, and *Today's FBI*, an internal employee magazine. Both periodicals were satisfactory, steady publications that I only read for the pictures.

During my earlier venture at the academy, I published a one-page rag on par with a high school production. I'd written articles over the years for magazines, including *The Enforcer*. That was the extent of my publishing experience. Despite my lack of credentials, I got the job—mainly because no one else wanted it.

The only tricky part was to get the Director to sign off on my transfer. He agreed to the deal since the publications office was just down the hall from the speechwriting office. I would be close by if the Director wanted me back—what we affectionately called a bungee-chord transfer.

When I walked into the publications office, I found a sleepy place. The staff of six people all had pulse beats below sixty, not because they didn't have the capability but because they hadn't been challenged in years. They knew what they were doing and had established a rhythm similar to the tempo of slow jazz music.

My predecessor was an attorney who was logical, steady, and traditional. I was none of these. So, off to the races.

I started to move out furniture and move in paintings, hold meetings and brainstorming sessions, ask many questions, and change how we did business. By the way, the advice I'd now give my former self would be "slow your role." But that's 20-20 hindsight. Instead, I charged ahead.

In short, I drove the staff nuts. "It's not intentional," I told everyone. To which one wag quipped, "Neither is an old lady who runs you over in her two-ton car because she didn't see you."

The first place I visited was the graphic designer's office; an operation stuck deep in the early 1900s. "Dan," who worked like a monk, toiled over a drafting table, using an Exacto knife and rubber glue to construct a handmade layout. I asked Dan many questions, the primary one being, "Why the hell don't you use a computer to lay out this magazine?" A pleasant guy, Dan answered each question patiently. He returned like an excellent elf to his drafting table when we finished.

The next day, I returned to Dan's office and wheeled in a computer borrowed from the technical services division. Dan was shocked and amazed that I had been able to secure this equipment and horrified that he'd have to master it quickly. The look on

Dan's face was priceless. He was unsure whether to smile or cry. Eventually, he did both.

The managing editor, "Kelly," had been around a long time. At first, she saw me like so many others in the Bureau did: a loose cannon, seemingly changing for change's sake.

Just as Elizabeth Kubler-Ross, author of *On Death and Dying*, identified the five stages of grief—denial, anger, bargaining, depression, and acceptance—Kelly went through the same stages to become "Gladiciszed," as she called it. Once she reached the final step—acceptance—we started to understand and appreciate each other.

Kelly saw that while I might be a bit of a nut, I made sense on some level, especially after a few beers. We began to laugh at each other and eventually became great friends and partners in the publishing process.

One of my first goals was to conduct a readership survey for *The Enforcer*, which had never been done. I figured it was a good idea to find out what our readers thought about the magazine, even though it was free to any police department that wanted it.

The research field has an old saying: You look for a mouse and find an elephant. We surveyed to determine which sections our readers preferred and which we should dump. The findings were ho-hum, but we found an unexpected elephant: Out of the magazine's one hundred thousand recipients, fully twenty-five percent were no longer in law enforcement or deceased.

Falling in the category of "I'd rather be lucky than smart," our elephant finding surfaced simultaneously as a movement to trim back government freebies. Faced with a shrinking budget, we considered many options: reducing the size of the magazine (already only thirty-two pages) but with no ads; trimming back on staff (never popular in group discussions); and donating part of my paycheck to the magazine (never popular with my Donna, who paid the bills).

Then it came to me in a vision or a nightmare: get rid of the over twenty-five thousand magazine recipients who were dead, retired, or in another post-retirement career. What kept me from acting immediately was the potential backlash from the retired agents, many of whom saw the magazine as a lifelong birthright.

So, I consulted a friend, an academic who studied the art of persuasion. He advised cutting all twenty-five percent; if anyone complained, add them back. His theory: you'd still get rid of a boatload of freeloaders.

It took me a couple of months of thinking and talking to folks before I lowered the boom. But we eventually cut a quarter of our subscribers. Sure, we got a few "what-the-hell-is-going-on" phone calls to which we said, "Oops, no problem, we'll put you back on the list." But in the end, we chopped thousands and reduced our costs by twenty-five percent.

One fellow who retired many years ago called and confessed to not reading the magazine for decades. "Ya got me," he said. "But I've been giving it to my nephew, who became a cop."

29

A Minnow Eats a Whale

As any business school student can explain, mergers and acquisitions don't happen quickly. About two-thirds of them end up in the toilet. Likewise, any marriage counselor will tell you that marriages also hit the commode with a frequency of fifty percent.

Internal mergers in the FBI weren't any picnic, either. I experienced this firsthand when the Bureau's elite and small Congressional Affairs Office merged with the much larger Office of Public Affairs. It was like watching a minnow eat a whale.

After the merger, Congressional Affairs (the minnow) became the dominant team, and Public Affairs (the whale) became the subservient team. It was a winner versus losers, in-group versus out-group situation.

Almost overnight, I found myself in the out-group: Public Affairs. Many of us whale remnants were not treated maliciously but with polite, benign neglect.

For example, let's say I got to attend a meeting. Our leader, "Colin," might ask, "Who has any thoughts on whether the Director should speak at the annual 4-H convention in Kansas?"

Joe Congressional Affairs: "I think it's a great idea. All those cows will make the Director look more human."

Colin: "Good thought. I like that line of perception. Cows do offset the Director's serious demeanor and, at the same time, lend themselves to making him look like he has those solid, Midwestern values. Very good. Anyone else?"

I raise my hand.

"Anyone else?"

I wave my hand.

Colin looks way to the right of me.

I speak up.

"Colin, I have a thought."

"Oh, of course. I must have missed you."

"The Director and cows, I think, might send the wrong message. Besides, who the hell would ever book a speech with 4-H? What a goofy idea. Really!"

"I did," Colin says. "Any other new business before we adjourn?"

I'm toast.

After this type of exchange happened a few more times, I became moldy toast. That's when the FBI announced another one of its arbitrary personnel policies for which it had become infamous.

Under this new "brilliant" policy, some senior headquarters experts transferred into field jobs for which they were no longer suited. Others in the field moved against their will back to headquarters to do jobs for which they were unqualified and had no interest. It was a form of musical chairs designed by a masochist.

Now that I was a member of the "out-group," I knew what would happen when the now-combined Office of Congressional and Public Affairs had to offer up its sacrificial lambs. It would take less time to say "Bye, bye" before my name would join the other older Public Affairs misfits bounced out of headquarters.

As the storm clouds gathered, I decided to evacuate to safer ground.

It had always been my dream to end my career at the FBI Academy, and because I would always be out of step in the Bureau's parade, the likelihood of returning to the academy one last time was high. I'd say, "Get thee to the Academy—fast this time."

As it turned out, "Nick," an old friend and former Public Affairs colleague, was now at the academy. A guy with the same personality disorder as me—namely that he was a step or two out of sync with the rest of the FBI's precision marching band—Nick understood me as well as anyone, and still, he liked me.

First, I gathered all the folks in the magazine unit and asked how many would consider moving to the academy. About two-thirds agreed.

I proposed the move first to Nick, who thought it a great idea. The academy, however, was also caught up in the transfer of older agent instructors back to the field for temporary or permanent assignments. Under the circumstances, he cautioned, it would take a real magic trick to transfer the magazine staff, but if anyone could make chicken salad from chicken shit, it was me.

Reaching deep into my bag of career-advancement tricks, I pulled out an old tactic that worked the last time I got sent (bounced) to the academy: the "push-me-pull-me" technique.

I wrote a white paper that I showed to Nick, my advocate, and Colin, my current boss. In all likelihood, Colin would never read past the white paper's executive summary, which laid out an iron-clad rationale for placing the magazine—which was all about training—at the training academy.

Knowing I was leaving one way or the other, Colin approved my recommendation to transfer the magazine staff to the academy—the push-me part of my tactic. At the other end, the pull-me part happened when Nick approved and forwarded the recommendation to the administrative folks, who supported it without question.

The push-me-pull-me tactic had worked again.

The Misfit Chief Speechwriter—Key Takeaways

Give misfits a chance to earn your trust. Once established, please give them a loose leash and let them do their thing. My deviation from a long-entrenched speech-writing procedure gained the support of my new boss—not a small accomplishment, given that he and I started on tentative ground.

Supply ample tech support. No creative oddball can operate to full potential without current technology. Don't make them fight for it. And if you think holding onto rickety computers "saves money," think again—the lost productivity results in the opposite.

Make everyone feel included. No one on your team should ever be made to feel like a second-class citizen. No one on your team should be allowed to act like a prima donna. As part of my misfit leadership style, I insisted that we all sink or swim together.

The Not-So-Misfit FBI Academy Unit Chief

30

Back to La-La Land— This Time by Choice

Quietly, the magazine team packed up and moved to the FBI Academy. The academy's new assistant director wore a perplexed, slightly annoyed expression as he stood and watched the small parade of moving boxes enter the building.

"What's this?" he asked.

Nick acted surprised when he showed the transfer document to the assistant director. Then he glanced my way and winked at me. The transfer, I'm sure, added to a growing tiff between Nick and the assistant director, his new, pain-in-the-ass boss. It was an act of courage that likely accelerated the ending of Nick's tenure at the academy.

The transfer immediately triggered a requirement to combine my magazine group with the teaching unit I had been an instructor in during my previous stint at the academy. The merger resulted in a new, large unit that published a magazine, taught new agents and law enforcement leaders, and conducted communication and leadership training for experienced agents in the field.

Managing the merger was a tall order, but it fit well with my track record of overseeing initiatives for which I had no experience. I took it on like a one-hundred-fifty-pound rookie defensive cornerback goes after a two-hundred-fifty-pound all-pro fullback.

Not everyone was overjoyed with the new arrangement. The magazine folks first saw the transfer to the academy through rose-tinted sunglasses. Once they started their commutes to the academy, forty or fifty miles away for some of them, attitudes chilled like a cup of coffee set by an open window in winter.

On the other side were the instructors and support staff from the teaching group, a well-entrenched team that hadn't had a permanent leader for months. Now, a former colleague they knew as a rookie had jumped ahead in the line of succession.

As the new leader, I had to make this shaky merger work. So, I spent much time showing the two sides how they could help each other succeed.

To the instructors, I explained how the magazine team would help them publish, a bothersome requirement for many faculty members. For some, writing was a four-letter word beginning with F—Fear. Having a group of expert writers on hand to help tune up—and likely ghostwrite—a piece for publication was particularly persuasive.

On the other hand, the magazine staff often had to scour the field to find a cop willing to write and submit an article. The notion of having a ready source of authors within arm's reach had strong appeal.

Based on these complementary needs, I launched my campaign to win the hearts and minds of the two factions. I won't say it was easy, but I was determined to integrate them over time.

I also had to integrate the instructors, who had their pecking order. Some taught new FBI agents; others instructed veteran police officers in the National Academy. The position of the new-agent instructor was often assigned to new arrivals to the instructional team as a proving ground for instructors. If the new-agent instructors did well, they were allowed to teach in the more elite National Academy.

Sometimes you get lucky and unlucky simultaneously, like when you win the lottery or get promoted (both can bring simultaneous joy and pain along life's bumpy road). I was lucky when the Director mandated a new agent's training change. For years, Training had produced only a trickle of new agents to replace sluggish retirement. Under the mandate, we would have to train at levels that would eventually approach one thousand new agents yearly.

This warp-speed ramp-up was viewed as nothing short of outrageous by all the teaching groups at the academy. It would require accelerating at an order of magnitude of gearing up for World War II.

For me, the Director's demand was good news. It was my excuse to create a curriculum war room.

On the day we heard about the mandate, I met with all faculty members within our unit that afternoon. I told them that we had to revise and refresh our curriculum—part of the Director's mandate—and that every agent instructor would teach at least one section of the curriculum for new agents. Period. No exceptions.

I also informed the group that they were now a task force responsible for revising the entire new-agents curriculum within the next three weeks. I then appointed "Sam," an experienced, talented, and dependable instructor, as the task force leader.

Then I left the room. Once outside, I heard the loud discussion, doors slamming, and some creative profanity.

But the mandate stood. I'd learned from years of success and failure that the best thing you can do is ride the wave. A CEO once told me, "Never waste a good crisis." I planned to use this one to unite the instructors, like it or not.

31

Educators Run Amok

Soon after that initial meeting, the leaders from each teaching group gathered around a large conference table. Because of the torrent of new agents who'd soon be roaring through the system like a tidal wave, we needed a plan to recruit a batch of new instructors from the field—and pronto. We also needed to know the requirements of our faculty as we prepared to redesign the new agent's curriculum.

Sam, the guy I appointed as the task force leader, went around the table and asked each of us what we wanted to see in the curriculum. Not surprisingly, each teaching unit pushed its favorite training. "They need more law." "They need to write better." "They need management skills." "They need _____ (fill in the blank)." The curriculum wish list began to look like a Christmas tree.

Earlier in my career, I might have endured a bidding-style method to design a course. In recent years, I returned to school and received a doctorate in education and human development. Now I had little tolerance for laundry lists or turf battles that pushed important content off the table.

For a task like curriculum development, you'd think someone with the knowledge needed to get the job done would be welcomed with open arms. But that wasn't the case in the FBI. If you asserted your expertise, you'd be chastised for being a know-it-all. You'd also be assured of never being invited back for another meeting.

While the conversation around the table was entertaining, I felt morally obligated to stop this curriculum development rollercoaster ride from hell. I also knew picking the right approach was critical.

So, I played the only card I knew would stop the show: a prospective lawsuit.

During my many years in education, I'd learned that whenever you wanted to put the brakes on educators run amok, all you had to do was raise the possibility of litigation. No other institution seemed to be as sensitive to lawsuits as the FBI, especially when I was an agent. Back then, the Bureau was rife with class action suits from women and minorities.

"What about the HR Report?" I said in a deep, official-sounding voice.

I'm using a fictitious name but "the HR Report" was an actual report that hit the Bureau like a freight train. People around the table looked at me as if I had just asked them to solve Fermat's theorem or explain Einstein's theory of relativity.

"What report?" asked one colleague who was brave enough to voice the question on everyone's mind.

"The HR Report, which perhaps a few of you may know about," I said, pausing to let that line sink in.

"The HR Report," I continued, "was a direct response from a class action lawsuit filed on behalf of a woman who'd challenged the FBI's training," I mentioned the woman's name. Everyone nodded almost in unison, no doubt recalling the rather public groin kick of bad publicity brought by that particular lawsuit.

Now that I had the attention of these folks, I decided to conduct a short course on curriculum development. As a misfit agent with sand kicked in his face for pursuing his doctoral education instead of hot pursuit of field assignments, I savored the opportunity to kick sand onto some of these bullies.

"The report is a thousand pages and details the tasks performed by an FBI agent," I said. "A task analysis, if you will."

Most people in the conference room did not know what a task analysis entailed or why it was critical—ironically—to our task at hand. This time, I didn't wait for someone to ask.

"A task analysis breaks down a job into all its critical steps. For example, if you had to tell someone how to make a peanut butter sandwich, they'd have to know where to get the knives, unscrew the peanut butter jar top, open the bread, spread the peanut butter, and so on."

"What the hell? New agents and making peanut butter sandwiches?" one guy piped up.

I counted to five, collected myself, and said, "Just an example."

"Huh."

I moved on. "The consultants who wrote the HR Report determined what an agent did by interviewing hundreds of agents, supervisors, ASACs, and SACs."

I explained, step by step, how the consultants identified the critical elements that went into making a good FBI agent. "If you take each sub-step like writing reports, interviewing, knowing the law, being able to fire a weapon, using handcuffs, and the many other tasks named in the report, you have the basis for our new agents curriculum," I said.

As my tutorial continued, I saw some eyes start to glaze over. So, I cut to the chase.

"In short, we either use this report as the basis for our work, or we all get our asses sued off."

That did it. Attention gained.

32

The Colored Polo Shirt Phenomenon

Basic group theory says that groups will form, storm, norm, and perform. That's what happened within the new agents curriculum planning task force.

The storm part was the loudest. Lots of angst, chatter, threats, name-calling, finger-pointing, foot stomping, lip pouting, arm folding, eye rubbing, heart pounding, lip syncing, you name it. "I can't. I won't. We shouldn't. It wouldn't. They can't. They mustn't. When the group first received its assignment, they can't, can they?" were among the protests.

But after three weeks, the task force produced a new curriculum for new agent training that used the HR Report as its foundation. In the following months, we used the curriculum to position the FBI to handle the Director's highly ambitious mandate.

New FBI agents weren't the only students in law enforcement who received training at the Quantico Marine Corps Base. Sometime in the 1980s, the Drug Enforcement Administration (DEA) moved its new agent operation from the Federal Law Enforcement Center in Brunswick, Georgia, to Quantico.

As I mentioned, the FBI Academy and Training Division also operated the FBI National Academy. The officers and law enforcement managers accepted into this program came from all over the world—from Colombia to Japan, Nigeria to Brazil. Within the United States, the hometowns ran the gamut. Big cities like

Boston, Austin, New York, and Miami. Small towns in Kansas, Montana, Wyoming, and Nevada.

My return to the academy reintroduced me to this rainbow, whose rich, varied colors and dialects sharpened, and even hardened, the FBI Academy and Training Division's system of pedagogical segregation: the colored polo shirts.

I've been too lazy to track down the origins of the colored polo shirt phenomenon. But in my mind, its source is less important than its effect. The uniforms began to segment the academy and made it easy to typecast its participants.

In the FBI, the training atmosphere was more like a graduate school than a boot camp. The nonteaching staff, faculty, and students all respected each other. Questions and answers were more about clarification than permission and learning than recognizing rank. To complement its collegial approach to training, the FBI opted for a blue polo shirt with khaki pants, almost a preppy look that you might see at the University of Virginia.

The DEA had a completely different philosophy regarding teaching new agents, opting for a West Point look that supported the agency's hard-ass training mentality. Agents dressed in grey polo shirts emblazoned with the letters of their acronym. Black cargo pants bloused into polished black-leather combat boots completed the military-like ensemble. They were a study in black and grey, something Picasso might have loved in his grey period.

The dress code for National Academy cops underwent some laughable twists and turns. Several years ago, an administrator with a penchant for discipline decided that National Academy students could be better controlled by placing them in uniforms—and tacky ones. After much thought about how to transition these students from civilian attire to uniforms, the powers that be decided to ease them into the uniform mode by dressing each NA student in black shoes, khaki pants, and fire-engine red polo shirts bright enough to be seen from the moon with a pair of opera glasses.

"Hideous" would be the word I'd choose to describe both the decision and the shirt color. Putting senior law enforcement officers in buster-brown clodhopper shoes, tan knickers, and a lightbulb for a shirt made me laugh my pedagogical self silly.

To add insult to injury, most of these officers, now walking around in clown suits, were away from home for the first time. They had never done their laundry before, meaning they didn't know to separate their white underwear from their red shirts before putting their clothes in the wash. If you entered the gym locker room, you'd see a battalion of these poor saps walking around in pink underwear.

Thank God for a new administrator with a more compassionate strain who eventually took over the National Academy. While he didn't rescind the boy-scout outfits, he dared to change the shirt color from fire-engine red to hunter green. The resulting light green underwear seen in the locker room was a far cry from the pink of yesteryear.

While the students wore different colored shirts, the staff wore suits. It was easy to identify people and stereotype them immediately. Whenever we had everyday events in the auditorium, you could pick out the gangs by the shirts they wore.

The gangs were relatively cordial with each other. But unwritten rules existed about staying off each other's dorm floors and sitting in specific seats in the cafeteria, about who said hello first in the corridors, and when to acknowledge other academy gangs in civilian clothing.

The unwritten rules were strictly enforced and, for the most part, followed. No one wanted to be a misfit, "the fish that swam funny."

33

The Commandant of Snow Removal

Between implementing the revised curriculum for new FBI agents training and overseeing the merged magazine writing/teaching unit, I logged ultra-long days, as usual. During that time, the seasons passed quickly. Winter arrived once again at the academy. That prompted the SAC in Charge to issue an explicit, weather-related order: All staff members were to report to work, regardless of snow, sleet, hail, floods, hurricanes, tornados, earthquakes, or whatever.

If you were an essential instructor, you were expected to anticipate bad weather—and plan accordingly. That meant finding a way to get to the academy and being prepared to teach the trapped students lest they burn the place to the ground after a day or two of cabin fever.

The mid-Atlantic region, where the academy is located, has one of the iffier, less-predictable climates. Canada's arctic stream can quickly dip into our area, giving us sub-teen temperatures. The Gulf Stream might stop by for an extended visit, making it feel like spring. And when these two extremes happen to form a meteorological sandwich, it's the perfect setup for an ultra-bad winter storm.

That happened one February night during the year I was scheduled to retire—my last winter at the FBI Academy.

My family and I had tickets for a local concert this evening. I planned for the worst in response to dire snow warnings—and with the SAC's show-up-no-matter-what-the-hell-happens order deeply set in my mind. We took two cars to the performance, with mine packed with extra clothes, my overnight stuff, and all my work paraphernalia.

During the concert's intermission, I checked the parking lot. It was covered with almost an inch of snow which, in Washington, was enough to drive hundreds of thousands of people immediately to the supermarket to buy the big three: milk, bread, and toilet paper. It was also enough to cause panicked drivers to begin skidding off the roads.

As the weather warnings escalated, I made my decision. Like a soldier off to war, I kissed Donna and my daughters goodbye and headed to the academy on a Saturday night.

The visibility was like being in a pillow fight after a busted pillow released a thousand white feathers. Knowing that the side roads are always the first to get slippery, I headed south on Route 95. Several cars had already skidded onto the highway's shoulder and sat at interesting angles like game tokens tossed haphazardly from a giant Monopoly board.

I gritted my teeth, clenched the steering wheel, and leaned forward to see out the windshield. The trip took over an hour and a half, about twice as long as usual. When I exited onto the Marine base roads, I prayed that my ancient Honda Civic would come through for me. Thankfully, it did after a dozen white-knuckled spins and skids around twists and turns that were tricky to negotiate on a clear day.

Not long after I arrived, I noticed the SAC's car pull in, which made me feel smug about the conversation I'd had with Donna at the concert. "Why do you think you need to leave?" she asked. "Are you sure it wouldn't make sense to let the plows work all night and set out tomorrow?"

As usual, Donna's thinking was reasonable, but it sounded pure nonsense to me then. And now that I had made it in, I could only think of calling her to proclaim, "See? I'm not the only person paranoid enough to show up on Saturday night!"

The snow continued to fall with force seldom seen in our area. By Monday morning, we had well over two feet, an almost unheard-of amount that put the weather geeks into orbit.

That morning, the SAC called a meeting with everyone who was there—a handful of neurotics like me, plus a dozen or so duty agents and security people who'd been trapped in the academy over the weekend. We huddled in the auditorium to discuss how we'd conduct classes.

We decided to cancel the National Academy police training but hold new FBI agents training. That way, we could say we were operational—however questionable that statement might be. It was all about perception, not reality.

The instructors held a few half-hearted classes attended by roughly fifty new agents stuck at the academy. Since most of us had never taught new agents, we told war stories and held student breakout discussions on random problem-solving topics (such as how you might clear the academy from being snowbound?). After a while, we halted the instruction and focused on the critical task: digging ourselves out from the snowbound academy covered in a couple of feet of snow.

We gathered once again in the auditorium. By now, we had a larger crowd of the new agents and anyone else interested in our next survival steps.

At one point, I suggested getting one or two helicopters and using them like giant snowblowers to remove the tons of snow on the academy's flat-as-a-pancake roofs before they began to collapse. I thought this was one of my more brilliant ideas. The SAC did not.

After that suggestion, I was placed in charge of the shoveling detail. Along with the fifty new agents, we set out to the task.

The maintenance guys called to tell us where to find tools. Before long, we'd armed each snow soldier with snow shovels, cafeteria trays, and anything that could be used to push tons of snow. After several hours, the only thing we accomplished was clearing all the doors in case of fire; beyond that, we got a bunch of exercise and more laughs than grown adults should be allowed.

I didn't get my car dug out until Thursday, when all classes resumed. By then, I had been officially added to the academy's book of folklore as "The Commandant of Snow Removal."

And to this day, whenever we get belted by a big snowstorm, it triggers memories of my suggestion to use helicopters as snowblowers. I still think the idea has some merit.

The Not-So-Misfit FBI Unit Chief—Key Takeaways

Watch out for hidden pecking orders. When I returned yet again to the FBI Academy, I merged the magazine team with the teaching group, which had its system for ranking instructors. Upper management isn't always aware of these pecking orders, which can wield power. A department or individual office with an internal pecking order can result in an oddball employee being ostracized, even if the organization at large promotes a culture of acceptance.

Be aware of the pros and cons of "uniforms" in the workplace. By uniforms, I'm referring to any "preferred clothing" worn by everyone in the office. On the positive side, uniformity makes everyone equal. And on the negative side, uniformity ... makes everyone similar! Uniformity is likely a total turnoff for misfits, oddballs, and nonconformists because uniformity suppresses employee individuality.

Don't be a know-it-all. You could earn this label—and maybe get booted off the team or a project— if you assert your expertise too quickly or strongly. As one FBI Agent said," Don't be a sexual intellectual ... A F—ing Know-it-all!" To be an accepted and valued contributor, listen first and ask thoughtful questions. Show equal respect for everyone regardless of stature or educational level.

The Misfit Agent Waves Goodbye

34

Saying Goodbye Ain't So Easy

In every career, there's an optimal time to say goodbye. But most people, especially FBI agents, stay too long on the farm.

I've watched people with significant accomplishments and reputations wither and die on the vine. They become cranky old farts, talking about the good old days. How good things used to be. How new agents and, consequently, the new Bureau were collectively going to hell in a handbasket.

The FBI set the mandatory retirement for agents at age fifty-seven, supposedly for administrative reasons. But I believe it's because aging agents are such a pain in the ass that the Bureau would rather pay them in retirement than listen to all their grousing.

I was better than most at closing doors and opening new ones, a likely byproduct of my misfit nature. My wife claims that if anyone can do it, I'll be the one who shows up early for my funeral.

Whatever the reason, in January 1996, I submitted my resignation effective on July 2, the day after my fiftieth birthday. Age is one-half of the two magic FBI agent retirement components; the other is years of service. In my case, my age (fifty) and my twenty years of service equaled seventy years. That simple-but-powerful equation opened the door to a lifelong pension and guaranteed health care, not to mention the right to tell some inflated stories distorted by the mercy of passing time and failing memories.

Like many people, I'd like to think that I was irreplaceable. One FBI old-timer helped me come to grips with reality. "Thrust your fist into a pale of water and then pull it out quickly," he said. "The length of time that there's a gaping hole before the water fills it is the length of time it will take them to get along without you."

Soon after that conversation, I started cleaning out cabinets filled with years of old accumulated memorabilia, like the plastic razorback hog statue I received from a police school at the University of Arkansas (the home of the Razorbacks). I tossed out tons of photos taken when I taught at police schools in various cities—Cleveland, Houston, Memphis, New Orleans, and Cincinnati, among other spots.

In the FBI, saying goodbye is a process that starts the day you turn in your letter of resignation. It takes roughly twenty-four hours for everyone who knew you to hear the news through "the grapevine," a much faster and more efficient informal communication system than any official notification. Like a jailbreak, the remaining inmates are happy for you but mad that you've escaped, leaving them behind.

The ritual of separation from the FBI requires that you have the same conversation over and over about one thousand times before you leave. My separation conversation tango went something like this.

"Hey, I hear you're retiring."
"Sure am. In July."
"What are you going to do?'
"Looking at a couple of jobs."
"Doing security work?"
"Nope."
"Really? What then?"
"Probably something in PR or teaching."
"Really?"

Many agents have difficulty conceptualizing a post-retirement job that doesn't include investigations. Because I wasn't much of an investigator as an agent, I couldn't imagine that I'd suddenly have an epiphany. Moving toward a different light made sense to me but not to others with whom I'd been a misfit for over twenty years.

Like most of my career, my departure process was different. For one thing, I gave six months' notice. Most agents avoid giving notice too far in advance to conserve power for longer. By contrast, I wanted to become a lame duck quickly. I reasoned that giving up control and responsibility would allow me to job hunt with gusto.

In the months before I retired, my unit produced an entire spoof issue of our law enforcement magazine dedicated to my odd view of life. Some might view this production as a supreme act of love. And I'd like to believe that; however, an alternative theory might be that these poor folks had been so abused by my out-of-whack, abnormal, misfit FBI personality that my departure required a certain level of catharsis—and a way to rid themselves of me for once and for all.

As it turned out, my long lead time had another advantage. It provided plenty of time for anyone who wanted to take a well-thought-out shot at me at my retirement party.

And what a party it would turn out to be.

35

The Last Hurrah—Party Time

Most FBI retirement parties turn into a roast, where every faux pas you've ever made, every ball you've ever dropped, and every bureaucrat you've ever alienated is remembered in front of a gathering of friends and family. As the retiree, you're expected to crack a joke or two and then sentimentally thank the free world for all the help it's given you, take a bow, get your plaque, graciously accept a couple of gifts (one is usually a paperweight), and trundle off into the sunset—without badge or gun—to play shuffleboard or bridge.

In my case, I had to suffer public humiliation in front of approximately one hundred people in the Atrium of the Academy. People showed up from all of my previous jobs: from headquarters, from various field divisions, and of course, from the academy itself. My immediate family—Donna, our two girls, and Donna's parents—were also there to share in the public ridicule.

The emcee, "William," introduced my family and Donna, referring to her as Saint Donna. After softening up the crowd like a warm-up act in Vegas, he introduced a couple of agents who had worked with me in the past, both of whom took a few shots at me before saying some nice things.

William then introduced "Whitlow," the Agent in Charge of the FBI Academy, who had brought much-unwanted change management with him. Like many well-meaning administrators who had never been teachers or trainers, he had definite views of what academy teachers should do—much like people with no children who love to give you advice about raising yours.

Whitlow was brief but snuck in a couple of stock one-liners: "This is the first time anyone has paid for me to come to a retirement luncheon." Baddabing. And, "Steve didn't get ulcers; he gave them."Baddaboom! Whitlow then presented me with a display of historical FBI badges that was quite attractive. I wondered if I could put the collection in my car's rear window to forestall future speeding tickets.

The next speaker, Jack, was my first official training agent— the guy who asked me to watch Gerald, the underwear-clad probation fugitive. Jack recounted with exquisite detail how I watched Gerald walk down the stairs of his mother's two-story tenement, open the door, and sprint barefoot down the street in the dead of winter.

"We often thank families at this time for letting us have their spouses for all these years, and we give them back to you in retirement a little more tattered and worn," Jack told the crowd. "But in Steve's case, Donna thanked us for keeping him!"

"Amelia," a University of Virginia representative, took the mic and reminisced about our first meeting, which she described as "like nuclear energy." She recounted how my unit had the most people at every faculty development session held by the university, something she found very important. "If Jefferson were here, he'd be proud of Steve," she said. Amelia's praise was the highest I received that day. She presented me with a gorgeous print of the Rotunda, which still hangs in my office.

Then it was my turn. I had worked on my remarks like an entertainer trying a new bit for the first time. I thanked our speakers and folks at the front table and talked about a few bosses.

Borrowing a page from Dave Letterman's playbook, I listed the five reasons you know you're ready to retire.

Reason number five, you know it's time to retire when you don't know OR care who's on the FBI Career Board.

Reason four is that you read the federal column (which deals with pay raises and retirement information) more closely than the sports page.

Reason number three is that you know more people featured in *The Grapevine*, the FBI Society of Former Agents magazine, than in *The Investigator*, the FBI's employee magazine.

The number two reason is when you're older than the Director of the FBI.

And finally, the number one reason you know you are ready to retire from the FBI is when you're even older than the President of the United States (Bill Clinton). Badaboom!

After that, I turned a bit more serious—just for a minute or so—and explained what Quantico meant.

"Quantico has always been a touchstone for me, giving me what I needed when I needed it. In 1968, I came to Quantico to U.S. Marine Corps Officer Training School, and Quantico offered me a job right when I needed it. In 1970, after Vietnam, I returned to Quantico as a place to heal. They put me in charge of the officers club, and I turned it into a go-go joint by importing women from Mary Washington College and letting officers take off their jackets at informal night. I returned to Quantico in 1973 for FBI new agents training as Quantico gave me my first significant career as an FBI agent after being a Marine officer. In 1979, I came back as a public affairs officer. In 1983, I returned as an instructor, where I learned to teach, write, and find my true calling as a teacher and mentor. And finally, my last hurrah, I came back to Quantico in 1994 with the Publications Unit and was asked to combine it with my old unit—formerly the Education Communication Arts Unit ... and the melding of the two, while never easy, proved to be the capstone of my career, pulling together two groups that I loved so much."

For the most part, I kept the goodbye upbeat and funny to get through it without drawing a tear—especially my own. Then came the presentations of gifts. The most prized gift is my credentials and badge on a plaque showing my length of service from 1973 to 1996.

The kid pictured on my ID was the most interesting thing about this last gift. I had avoided updating my photo—and if anyone ever saw it, there was no way they would recognize me, except perhaps Donna. Taken over twenty-three years ago, the picture showed a strong, full-head-of-hair young Turk who stared confidently at me, now an older, wiser, slightly more bruised, more realistic, scarred, and experienced fifty-year-old guy who was ready to close one door and open another.

When the party was over, people shook my hand, wished me luck, trailed off, and spun back into their orbits, most of which would spin distinctly away from my own for the rest of my life.

I went to my now-former office, sat down, and felt the emotion drain out of my body. It felt like I had just run a marathon and finally could catch my breath. My family and closest friends had left, and I was alone in an empty office. All I could think was, "Thanks for letting me get through this."

36

The Day After

The morning after my retirement party, I got up early as usual and wandered down to the cave, my home office in the basement. I sat on the orange-print couch, thinking about the day before.

That's when it happened. I began to sob. I had maybe cried like this a half-dozen times in my life. It was deep, uncontrollable, and immensely satisfying when I finally stopped some five-to-ten minutes later.

The FBI mattered much more to me than I had ever realized—and when I finally left, it was as if I'd said goodbye to a wonderful friend. Despite our promise to stay in touch, we knew the theory of two planets spinning in separate orbits. Moreover, if we ever did see each other again, it would be stiffer, more formal, and more objective, like two old college friends at a reunion. My relationship with the Bureau would be forever different.

I thought deeper about what the FBI had meant to me—first, a hell of a meal ticket. Let's never underestimate the impact of a regular paycheck.

Second, the job's prestige gave me a great sense of pride. I'd always needed to be recognized, and whenever I said that I was an FBI agent, I got an awe-inspired reaction from people, except for criminals we'd come to arrest.

Third, the organization's size allowed me to gravitate to areas like the academy, where I felt most comfortable. A lesser organization would never have been able to allow the release valve I so much needed.

Finally, I loved the people of the FBI. Despite what you might read or envision on Hollywood screens, the FBI is made of people, salt-of-the-earth folks. There are some jerks, but every organization has "ten percenters." Simply put, ten percent of any group of people are jerks. But the other ninety percent, especially in the FBI, were the kind of folks you'd want looking for your kidnapped child, a terrorist bent on blowing up a building, or a white-collar criminal preparing to steal your aging mother's lifetime savings.

It had been a great run. I knew it and was very thankful, but it was time for this misfit FBI agent to move on. So, out loud to an empty room, after the tears dried up, I said, "Goodbye." Then I blew my nose.

The Misfit Agent Waves Goodbye—Key Takeaways

Gauge your last day with care. Like the rest of my FBI career, my departure was different. Most people don't need to give six months' notice like I did. On the other hand, the standard two weeks of notice isn't always enough. Adding more time may be good if a quicker departure jeopardizes key relationships or upends your team.

Give people the recognition they deserve. This includes introverts and the fish who dare to swim funny. No one wants to feel invisible or unappreciated. The recognition doesn't have to be a party if that isn't the style of the departing team member.

Don't settle for a traditional sendoff. I'll never forget the law enforcement magazine's two-page spoof issue that the editorial team produced in my honor. Be original. This is a big moment for the person who's moving on. The memory you create will last a lifetime.

Epilogue

After the FBI, I joined the University of Virginia (UVA) faculty, which had strong ties to the FBI because UVA accredited all the academic courses taught in the National Academy. I took the UVA job because of "Shirley," the dean at UVA. Shirley was a self-effacing, intelligent, and hysterically funny woman. I liked her and what she stood for—excellent adult education.

I ran UVA's extension campus in Northern Virginia for ten years. It was a real adjustment for me—and for them, I can assure you. My focus was on growth, and sometimes the speed I wanted did not match the more measured pace entrenched at the Northern Virginia center. We had a lot of fun, ups and downs, celebrations, and setbacks. Most importantly, we grew the center and staffed it with people who cared deeply about the University's mission.

But over time, I grew tired of running the center. The last straw was when a professor did something foolish: show hard-core porn to a class of mostly women, including a minister's wife, to demonstrate the latest uses of technology. I got rid of him after the semester following a blistering tongue-lashing and the installation of a monitor in his class.

I gave my boss six months' notice, about five months longer than it should have been. Being a lame duck that long felt like a holiday ornament on sale for fifty percent off the week after Christmas.

Fortunately, in my job as UVA's chief representative in Northern Virginia, I met a lot of great folks at a local Chamber of Commerce. So, I reached out to many of them and said I was looking for a change and to keep their eyes open.

That led to interviews with hiring managers who were my eldest daughter's age, then in her early thirties. Working with—let alone for—folks that age was about as appealing as being a substitute teacher in middle school.

So, I was done after my fifteenth interview with Gen Xers and, in some cases, millennials. That's when it came to me: if you don't like your job (or being offered), create your own.

So, after discussion, agreement, and backing from Donna, I decided to open up my own communications company that would focus on training, speaking, writing, and consulting. I went straight to what I knew and had taught for years: leadership communication skills. I had no idea what I was doing but had a laptop, a cell phone, and eventually an office. So, there I sat, feeling a bit lost but incredibly satisfied.

About two weeks into starting my company, I came home energized and said to Donna, "I'm finally in my own skin!" Honestly, it felt like what I thought it must be to come out as a gay man or woman. I hope I'm not minimizing or insulting the LGBTQ community, but finally, admitting what I loved to do and doing it was as liberating a thing as I've ever felt.

The company's reputation grew; over fifteen years later, I speak to business groups, train leaders, write books (like this one), and engage with my community by sitting on non-profit boards.

The decision not to expand and hire people was a conscious one. I did not want to be on the hook for young folks starting families and depending on my company for their livelihoods. I also hated the administrative duties of running that kind of company. Doing what I loved—and avoiding the administration I disdained—was significant. So, it became and remains a robust lifestyle business that allows me to be philanthropic, more politically engaged, and work with various other companies on a very comfortable ad hoc basis.

A year or so ago, I told Donna that if I died today, I'd view this last period as the icing on the cake. I'd have absolutely no regrets. A great place to be, I'd say.

Misfit Leadership: Key Takeaways

Overview

Our brains see the world in wildly different ways—and each of us has "a misfit streak," so to speak. If you nurture yours in a principled fashion, it will help you become a better leader. To practice misfit leadership, remember:

- Engage in self-learning

- Don't settle for the obvious

- Know your strengths and use them to find your tribe

- Understand that good stuff can happen from bad stuff

- Learn how to manage oddballs

The Misfit New Agent

Don't sweat the small stuff. Back when I was applying for the FBI, a small thing (my mustache) would have become a big thing if I hadn't shaved it off. Today, tattoos, multiple body piercings, and other displays of individuality have become more common in the workplace. Expect creative people to display their individuality and develop a policy that makes sense for your organization.

Watch out for rote onboarding. After a few dozen (or maybe a few hundred) briefings, people in charge of training can go on autopilot, like my bureaucratic "friend" Clyde. Encourage your trainers to exercise their inner weirdness and inject creativity into the onboarding process to keep it from getting stale.

Pair oddballs with mentors who "get" them. My partner Jack had no idea that—like many dyslexics—I tended to have a literal way of thinking. So when he asked me to "keep an eye on" the underwear man, that's precisely what I did—even as he sprinted barefoot down the street! To his credit, Jack laughed it off, and we developed a good relationship that lasted for many years.

The Misfit Language Student

Discourage groupthink. Groupthink happens when people who desire conformity make decisions without discussion or deliberation. That's basically what the "clagents" did when, as a group, they concluded that language school was a bad deal. To make matters worse, they kept their conclusion to themselves, which resulted in any dissenting agents (like me) unknowingly becoming misfits. Had their bosses intervened (or at least cared), this mindset could have been disrupted–and the language school might have been able to recruit more candidates.

Respect contrarians. I was one of the few agents who wanted to attend language school. I want to think that I showed a willingness to serve at a time when the FBI urgently needed foreign language proficiency. Appreciate the people in your organization willing to go against the grain and do what others don't (or won't) do.

Get to the root of head butting. When disputes arise between misfits and their bosses or coworkers, don't assume the problem rests with the misfit. In language school, I confronted "Professor Adolph" because I couldn't tolerate his sadistic treatment of the class and me.

The Misfit Field Agent

Tolerate weird routines. My running routine to train for the Boston Marathon was my form of mental therapy. Yes, it earned me a dubious nickname (The Rabbit). Still, it took place in the early morning, before my coworkers arrived at the office. Go with a weird routine if it makes your employee more productive and doesn't disrupt others.

Reward creativity that gets good results. The reward doesn't have to be financial (although it's nice when this happens). Often, it's enough to recognize and thank people for their unusual ideas and contributions.

Hear people out. You may decide an oddball's seemingly ridiculous idea is brilliant. At first, the hot dog-eating agents thought I was crazy when I suggested pitching a media story about their rescue of two scroungy mutts and their owner. Eventually, they agreed, and the pitch earned us some great press.

The Misfit Headquarters Agent

Assume good intent. My enthusiasm has always been my greatest asset—and my most significant liability. In hindsight, I now understand how I must have appeared despite my best intentions to make things work better, if not more creatively. If the misfits in your organization are rubbing people the wrong way, they're probably not doing it intentionally.

Listen to the message, not the tone. Misfits tend to have communication challenges. Many are overly introverted or extroverted (or blunt). You may learn something valuable if you ignore the noise and listen to their message.

Champion oddballs when they deserve your support. I landed a job promotion I wanted because I had three FBI career board members who stood up for me at a pivotal moment during a long, contentious discussion. Regarding the career paths of good team members who contribute to your organization, don't let quirkiness derail their progress. In the end, talent is talent, regardless of its wrapper.

The Misfit Field Supervisor

Leverage oddballs' strengths to get the best out of others—and vice versa. Pair misfits with partners who will grow and benefit from the oddball's creativity, a different perspective, and unique solutions to problems. When managed well, strange bedfellows can produce remarkable results.

Know the difference between power and authority. Power gives you the capacity to exert your will over someone else. Authority gives you the formal right to make decisions and issue commands. Most misfits don't do well under autocratic leaders who assert strong authority and expect unquestioning compliance and obedience from subordinates. Keep this in mind when assigning people to teams.

Learn people's backstories. An oddball's behavior will make more sense when you take the time to listen to their personal stories. You'll better understand why they do what they do.

The Not-So-Misfit Academy Instructor

Don't jump to conclusions about misfits. Sometimes they're just on the wrong bus or in the wrong place. They transform and thrive when moved to a department that's a better cultural fit or when they're allowed to work independently.

Be open to unconventional solutions. Admittedly, my decision to bait two tables of drunk patrons against each other wasn't a neat and pretty solution to the problem of clearing out in the FBI Academy's bar at the end of the night. But it worked. And no one got hurt!

Consider the opportunity cost of job promotions. If I hadn't accepted the job as chief speechwriter for the Director, I might have stayed fat, dumb, and happy at the academy. On the other hand, I might have stunted my career advancement had I turned down the job. Opportunity cost is a significant consideration for your talented misfits. If the promotion doesn't work out, they typically have a limited selection of places to go within your organization.

The Misfit Chief Speechwriter

Give misfits a chance to earn your trust. Once established, please give them a loose leash and let them do their thing. My deviation from a long-entrenched speech-writing procedure gained the support of my new boss—not a small accomplishment, given that he and I started on tentative ground.

Supply ample tech support. No creative oddball can operate to full potential without current technology. Don't make them fight for it. And if you think holding onto rickety computers "saves money," think again—the lost productivity results in the opposite.

Make everyone feel included. No one on your team should ever be made to feel like a second-class citizen. No one on your team should be allowed to act like a prima donna. As part of my misfit leadership style, I insisted that we all sink or swim together.

The Not-So-Misfit FBI Unit Chief

Watch out for hidden pecking orders. When I returned yet again to the FBI Academy, I merged the magazine team with the teaching group, which had its system for ranking instructors. Upper management isn't always aware of these pecking orders, which can wield power. A department or individual office with an internal pecking order can result in an oddball employee being ostracized, even if the organization at large promotes a culture of acceptance.

Be aware of the pros and cons of "uniforms" in the workplace. By uniforms, I'm referring to any "preferred clothing" worn by everyone in the office. On the positive side, uniformity makes everyone equal. And on the negative side, uniformity ... makes everyone similar! Uniformity is likely a total turnoff for misfits, oddballs, and nonconformists because uniformity suppresses employee individuality.

Don't be a know-it-all. You could earn this label—and maybe get booted off the team or a project— if you assert your expertise too quickly or strongly. As one FBI Agent said," Don't be a sexual intellectual ... A F—ing Know-it-all!" To be an accepted and valued contributor, listen first and ask thoughtful questions. Show equal respect for everyone regardless of stature or educational level.

The Misfit Agent Waves Goodbye

Gauge your last day with care. Like the rest of my FBI career, my departure was different. Most people don't need to give six months' notice like I did. On the other hand, the standard two weeks of notice isn't always enough. Adding more time may be good if a quicker departure jeopardizes key relationships or upends your team.

Give people the recognition they deserve. This includes introverts and the fish who dare to swim funny. No one wants to feel invisible or unappreciated. The recognition doesn't have to be a party if that isn't the style of the departing team member.

Don't settle for a traditional sendoff. I'll never forget the law enforcement magazine's two-page spoof issue that the editorial team produced in my honor. Be original. This is a big moment for the person who's moving on. The memory you create will last a lifetime.

About the Author

As one of the country's authorities on leadership, Dr. Steve Gladis coaches executives and their leadership teams to help them become more effective, collaborative, and positive. He is the CEO of Steve Gladis Leadership Partners, a Fairfax, Virginia-based leadership development company whose clients include a diverse mix of large and small businesses, associations, nonprofits, government agencies, and military organizations.

Dr. Gladis is the author of 27 books on leadership and communication, a senior scholar at George Mason University, and a speaker who regularly presents at conferences and corporate gatherings on leadership-related topics. A former faculty member at the University of Virginia, Dr. Gladis also served as an FBI special agent and was a decorated officer in the U.S. Marine Corps. In addition to his work in the leadership field, he is a novelist who writes stories based on his FBI career.

To contact Steve Gladis, please find him on LinkedIn or visit www.SteveGladisLeadershipPartners.com.

Other Leadership Books by Steve Gladis

The Four Critical Elements of a Great Team Leader

Leading Teams: Understanding the Team Leadership Pyramid

Leading Well: Becoming a Mindful Leader-Coach

Positive Leadership: The Game Changer at Work

Smile. Breathe. Listen.: The 3 Mindful Acts for Leaders

Self-Leadership: Become the CEO of Your Own Career

The Coach-Approach Leader: Questions, Not Answers, Make Great Leaders

The Trusted Leader: Understanding the Trust Triangle

The Journey of the Accidental Leader

The Executive Coach in the Corporate Forest

The Agile Leader: A Playbook for Leaders

The Transparent Leader: A Business Fable of Clear and Effective Leadership Communication

Novels by Steve Gladis

FBI Case: Quantico Kill

The Manipulation Project

Made in the USA
Middletown, DE
09 October 2023